The Mayflower Report, 1622

As Told by the Mayflower Pilgrims

Restored & Annotated

The
MAYFLOWER REPORT 1622

As Told by the Mayflower Pilgrims
William Bradford & Edward Winslow, et al.

Restored & Annotated

Illustrated with Engravings, Prints & Maps

David W. Bradford
Editor

Boston Hill Press

The Mayflower Report, 1622
Restored & Annotated
Copyright © 2007-2008 by David W. Bradford
Printed in the United States of America
All Rights Reserved

First Edition, 2008

This book is an original creative work
and is protected by copyright law.

Boston Hill Press
P.O. Box 215583
Town & Country Post Office
Sacramento, CA 95821

Library of Congress Catalog No. 2007930298
ISBN-13: 978-0-9787992-2-9, Softcover
ISBN-10: 0-9787992-2-4, Softcover

Printed & Distributed by
LSI
La Vergne, TN 37086

Previous Illustration:
Mayflower Pilgrims Pray Aboard Ship, 1620;
montage of a mural by Robert Weir, 1843.
(Author & Government Printing Office)

About the Original Authors

William Bradford (1590-1657) and Edward Winslow (1595-1655) were young friends who became leaders of the Mayflower Pilgrims. The two men were born to affluent families in Old England, but forsook wealth to seek reform of church and society.

As teenagers, both Messrs. Bradford and Winslow fled to Holland with the Pilgrim church to escape persecution by hostile English kings. The young exiles married fellow religious reformers and embarked on new careers. (William Bradford worked in the Dutch textile industry; Edward Winslow helped publish ground-breaking religious books.)

In 1620, though, the Pilgrim church decided to leave Holland, hoping for a fresh start in America. Messrs. Bradford and Winslow, along with their wives, joined the advance party, sailing aboard the tall-masted ship *Mayflower*. They were among 102 English emigrants, or Pilgrims, who hoped to build a new world amidst the unexplored wilderness that was then America.

However, starvation, a deadly epidemic, and warlike Indians threatened the would-be settlers. Messrs. Bradford and Winslow responded with exceptional courage; the Mayflower Pilgrims soon elected them as their leaders. For decades, the two friends amiably alternated as governors of Plymouth Colony. Together, they helped sow the seeds of a future nation—the United States of America.

Official Seal of Plymouth Colony

Contents

List of Maps 9
New Preface 11
New History of The Mayflower Report 13
New Format 19
New Note about Original Prefaces 21

[Original Title & Contents Page].............................23

[The Main Report]...25

    [*Episode I – Pokanoket*]...96
    [*Episode II – Nauset*]..108
    [*Episode III – Nemasket*].......................................113
    [*Episode IV - Massachusetts*]................................117

[*Appendix A* – First Thanksgiving]...........................122

[*Appendix B* – Reasons for America].......................129

[*Appendix C* – The First Preface] 139

[*Appendix D* – The Second Preface].........................141

[*Appendix E* – The Third Preface]...........................143

Index 149
Sources 151

List of Maps

New England, 1622-1644	24
John Smith's Map, 1614	26
Landfall at Cape Cod, 1620	27
Southern New England, 1634	35
Discovery of Plymouth Harbor, 1620	62
Plymouth Harbor (Detail)	63
Street Map of Plymouth, 1621	71
Boston Bay	117

New Preface

Nearly four-hundred years ago, the Mayflower Pilgrims fled persecution in England and set sail for the then mysterious land of America. They deliberately embarked on a great experiment—the building of a new, better world.

This book is their story, as told by the Pilgrims themselves. They related an often harrowing struggle in an untamed wilderness, but also boldly proclaimed discovery of what we now call the American Dream—a magical realm of breathtaking natural beauty and unlimited possibilities.

When first published in London in 1622, the Pilgrims' dramatic tale fascinated readers in a dreary post-medieval England: the Pilgrims did not just *describe* the distant new land that was then America; rather, they invited fellow idealists to *join* them and share in a wondrous new world.

No modern nation could have had a more purposeful chronicle of its earliest days. Nicknamed *Mourt's Relation*,[1] the Pilgrims' story inspired thousands of people to leave Old England and board ships for America, thereby beginning an historic migration.

Now that first report of the Pilgrims is again accessible to general readers. *The Mayflower Report, 1622* both restores and explains the original Pilgrim epic. Modern annotation and judicious editing make it one of the clearest versions ever. Once again, this book is the story that made America.

David Bradford
Editor

---

[1] *Mourt's Relation* is either a pun or a codename. See the following historical background and Appendix D.

A RELATION OR

Iournall of the beginning and proceedings of the English Plantation setled at *Plimoth* in NEW ENGLAND, by certaine English Aduenturers both Merchants and others.

With their difficult paſſage, their ſafe ariuall, their ioyfull building of, and comfortable planting themſelues in the now well defended Towne of NEW PLIMOTH.

AS ALSO A RELATION OF FOVRE
ſeuerall diſcoueries ſince made by ſome of the ſame Engliſh Planters there reſident.

I. In a iourney to PVCKANOKICK *the habitation of the Indians greateſt King* Maſſaſoyt : *as alſo their meſſage, the anſwer and entertainment they had of him.*

II. *In a voyage made by ten of them to the Kingdome of* Nawſet, *to ſeeke a boy that had loſt himſelfe in the woods : with ſuch accidents as befell them in that voyage.*

III. *In their iourney to the Kingdome of* Namaſchet, *in defence of their greateſt King* Maſſaſoyt, *againſt the* Narrohigonſets, *and to reuenge the ſuppoſed death of their Interpreter* Tiſquantum.

IIII. *Their voyage to the* Maſſachuſets, *and their entertainment there.*

With an anſwer to all ſuch obiections as are any way made againſt the lawfulneſſe of Engliſh plantations in thoſe parts.

LONDON,
Printed for *Iohn Bellamie*, and are to be ſold at his ſhop at the two Greyhounds in Cornhill neere the Royall Exchange. 1622.

*Original Title Page of the
First Report by the Mayflower Pilgrims
(Published in 1622 by John Bellamie of Cornhill, London.)*

New History of the Mayflower Report, 1622

The genesis of this book began on a little-remembered day in early December of 1621. At dawn, a wooden sailing ship, propitiously named the *Fortune*, hoisted her anchor from a shimmering bay on the coast of Massachusetts. The ship was alone; few vessels then dared so late in the year to ply the uncharted, shipwreck-littered waters of America.

Nevertheless, despite the risks, the *Fortune* had acquired a fine cargo of American furs and lumber. The vessel's billowy sails now caught a favorable wind, and her captain gladly set a course for the high seas of the Atlantic Ocean. The *Fortune* was bound for home —England—a journey of thousands of miles across open water.

Standing at the ship's railing and looking back at the receding shoreline was an aged passenger bundled up against the cold December breeze. He was Robert Cushman, the business agent for the cargo, and not the most obvious person to develop a great book about America. Mr. Cushman came over from England scarcely a month ago and was returning with the *Fortune*. In frail health, he had seen and done little during his brief visit to the New World.

His last glimpse of America, though, was a magnificent one. An aquamarine sea broke upon brilliant beaches and massive granite rocks that jutted into the sea. On shore, beyond the breaking waves, was a dense forest of pines, oaks, and other trees, some still flecked with the crimson and golden glory that is autumn in New England.

Indeed, Mr. Cushman's ship seemed insignificant against the raw beauty of the vast, untamed continent that was then America. Only scattered wisps of smoke, wafting up from beneath groves of towering pines, hinted at human activity upon the land—unseen Indians stoked campfires to ward off the morning chill.

Several columns of smoke, though, drifted from atop a prominent hill overlooking the shore. The haze came from the tree-shrouded chimneys of Plymouth Village, the already well-established home of the Mayflower Pilgrims.

Failure – However, Robert Cushman, the solitary passenger of the England-bound *Fortune*, scarcely noticed the view. He was lost in thought, being a man full of regrets. As a former official of the Pilgrim church, Mr. Cushman had been destined to be one of the most famous men in history. Instead, he was condemned to obscurity; Robert Cushman would not share in the *Mayflower's* glory.

Worse, he had only himself to blame; the Pilgrims originally invited him to join the *Mayflower's* voyage of 1620, then only a year past. Mr. Cushman was a deacon of their church and well-qualified to help build a religious colony. However, he became unexpectedly quarrelsome and complained of an ill-defined illness.

None spoke openly of cowardice; fear is deadly contagion, a risk to all on a dangerous expedition. Rather, in September 1620, just before the *Mayflower* sailed to America, Robert Cushman quietly disembarked. By mutual consent, he remained behind in England, joining others on waiting lists for future voyages.

A year later, in this autumn of 1621, Mr. Cushman finally caught a ride to America with the merchant ship *Fortune,* but only visited for a month. He was abruptly returning to England; he never again saw America.[1] By contrast, the Mayflower Pilgrims—and thousands of their followers—went on to immortal fame.

Inspiration – However, on this brisk December day of 1621, Robert Cushman likely had an inspiration: an unusual piece of cargo in his possession offered a rare second chance to make amends for failings; Mr. Cushman might yet redeem himself.

For the *Mayflower* colonists had shared with him a pleasant surprise: real-time written records of their adventure. Indeed, several Pilgrims had the foresight to keep daily journals. The authors entrusted Mr. Cushman with their handwritten notes for safekeeping; he was taking their personal papers back to England, along with the shipment of furs and lumber.

Those papers contained meticulous day-to-day accounts of the Pilgrims' first year in America (1620-1621). As fascinating as their story is to us now, it was infinitely so to Robert Cushman, the would-be Pilgrim. In riveting prose were vivid descriptions of un-

---

1 However, Robert Cushman left behind his young son, Thomas, to be raised by the Pilgrims in Plymouth. The family would be, forever more, American.

known rivers, forests, and exotic peoples, as well as an abundance of new animals and plants; the narratives were easily among the most complete accounts of the New World then in existence.

Moreover, the material had more than just literary value. The Pilgrims hoped to be trailblazers, lighting the way for other idealistic settlers to sail to America. A brilliant travelogue could inspire just such a mass migration and, hopefully, the seeds of a new society.

Publication – Mr. Cushman saw his opportunity. Upon returning to England, he quickly edited and arranged for publication of the Pilgrim journals. In 1622, only two years after the *Mayflower* sailed, the resulting book, *Mourt's Relation,* became a minor sensation.[1] America, the Pilgrims reported, was a fine place to live, not just for hardy explorers, but for everyday people of all walks of life.

Preparations for new expeditions to America commenced in earnest. These included the ambitious efforts of John Winthrop, a wealthy lawyer with many friends from the English town of Old Boston, a center of religious idealism. Using the Pilgrims' report as a guide, Mr. Winthrop and his friends organized a fleet of ships, packed with 1,000 colonists, ten times those of the *Mayflower*.

In 1630, the fleet sailed for America and arrived at an enormous natural harbor, recommended by the Pilgrims as an excellent place to live. The new colonists named the place, "Boston," after their former hometown in England. The settlers would be the vanguard of a Great Migration—over 20,000 sympathizers of the Pilgrims flocked to America in the following decades. Their "new England" quickly became one of the most prosperous, and dare one say, happy places on earth.

In storybook fashion, their offspring became the Founding Fathers (and Mothers) of a new nation—the United States of America. The Pilgrim dream of a new, better world was fulfilled; Robert Cushman had his redemption. As a friend later wrote, Mr. Cushman was "a special instrument" for the good of all.[2]

---

1 William Bradford and Edward Winslow, *et al.*, *A Relation or Journall* [sic] *of the beginning and proceedings of the English Plantation setled* [sic] *at Plimoth in New England* (London: John Bellamie, 1622).
2 William Bradford, *Bradford's History of Plymouth Plantation*, ed. William T. Davis (New York: Charles Scribner's Sons, 1908) p. 89.

Faded Legend – Robert Cushman's brainchild, *Mourt's Relation*, has seldom been out of print ever since. However, the book's unique origin ultimately dimmed its own popularity.

Fearing reprisal from a hostile English king,[1] Mr. Cushman discreetly disguised the Pilgrim manuscript. He cited the authors only by initials; fabricated an odd title, *Mourt's Relation*; and omitted the ship's name, *Mayflower,* and that her passengers were religious refugees.

In its early years, this disguise was no barrier to the popularity of the tale. By word-of-mouth, most knew that *Mourt's Relation* was the story of the Mayflower Pilgrims. (*Mourt* is an alias or pun. See Appendix D.)

However, memories faded with the passage of time, and the saga's ancient grammar slowly grew impenetrable. Most eventually forgot that *Mourt's Relation* was code for the *Mayflower* epic. By the late-nineteenth century, copious footnotes were required to understand the narrative, and the book quietly receded from the America it helped to create.

Great Story – In recent decades, *Mourt's Relation* returned as a niche curiosity, an opportunity to marvel at the "quaintness" of the Pilgrims and their outdated grammar. However, only the English language had changed, not the Pilgrim story.

And what a story the Pilgrims had to tell. Their expedition unexpectedly encountered terrifying storms, bitter cold, deadly disease, gnawing hunger, and fierce combat with Indians. Half of the settlers perished; the survivors were fortunate even to be alive.

The Pilgrims, though, were undaunted. For through their travails, they discovered a life-giving treasure in America—an unprecedented natural wealth of verdant forests, flourishing wildlife, and teeming seas—all scarcely noticed by previous explorers.[2] America could be a new Garden of Eden, a wilderness that was not so much threatening, as it was unharvested.

Indeed, a wondrous paradise of plenty beckoned. Sweet freshwater, wild fruits, fish, fowl, deer, and even whales—all could be

---

1   King James persecuted the Pilgrims for advocating religious reform.
2   Most explorers sought quick wealth as gold and silver, or worse, through enslavement of the natives. The Pilgrims ignored such dubious treasure.

easily had. The soil was rich and endless, well suited for crops of the Old and New Worlds. Even the much dreaded "salvages," i.e., the Indians, were not as hostile as they first appeared. Many tribes were friendly, and diplomacy could tame even the most warlike.

This vision of an idyllic wilderness became the cornerstone of an American dream: All life's needs could be satisfied from the good earth, a magic kingdom available to all.

Or put another way, the Pilgrims created a new definition of wealth, one that would change world history. Wealth was not lifeless scraps of paper and metal, i.e., money; rather, a supreme abundance of nature was the true treasure, providing all people with the necessities of life. Such real wealth could end all hunger and poverty—there would never again be destitute peasants or beggars.

In short, America could be a promised land, a new Zion.

The Authors – This momentous possibility was well documented by the Pilgrims themselves, primarily Edward Winslow and William Bradford, both future governors of Plymouth Colony. No nation could have asked for better founders—or reporters.

Messrs. Winslow and Bradford had gifted pens, crafting brisk narratives of the *Mayflower* adventure. Four centuries later, their tale remains irresistible: A small band of refugees escape to a mysterious land filled with exotic plants, animals, and mysterious natives—the Indians.

Edward & Elizabeth Winslow
Author & Wife

That said, the Pilgrim authors wrote under difficult circumstances, and their writing reflects it. They were often ill, cold, or hungry. They jotted notes only in their spare time, being otherwise burdened by the minutiae of administering a precarious colony.

As such, their writing does not have the same clarity as the *King James Bible* or other great literary works of the era. The Pilgrims often made only truncated entries with basic facts omitted. Their grammar, spelling, and punctuation were erratic; run-on sentences and incomplete thoughts were all too frequent.

To compound the problem, the original publisher of 1622, John Bellamie of London, introduced more errors. He struggled to read the handwritten manuscript and misprinted it; the Pilgrim authors, away in America, were unable to make corrections.

As such, the verbatim report is exceptionally difficult for modern readers. Archaic grammar mingles with misprinted words and cryptic clauses; the text frequently suggests meanings very different from the authors' intent.

Editorial Challenge – Nevertheless, a rough narrative also reflects reality, echoing a life-and-death struggle in a harsh wilderness—that tone cannot be easily altered, even in the interest of readability. Hence, the challenge is to refresh and clarify the Pilgrim text, without disturbing the emotional impact of the story.

Several methods of restoration are possible. One approach might be to completely rewrite the Pilgrim tale, using up-to-date grammar and vocabulary. However, for reasons mentioned, this would unduly alter the tale's dramatic quality.

Alternatively, one could preserve the ancient text and use footnotes to explain puzzling passages. However, such an approach is very cumbersome. (An edition printed in 1865 had hundreds of footnotes, whose total verbiage exceeded the original text itself.)

Old and New – This edition takes a new, different approach, one that preserves *and* modernizes the Pilgrim tale. Explanatory clauses and annotations are inserted *into the original narrative* with only a minimum of footnotes. In addition, spelling, punctuation, and format are updated and rectified.[1] (See the New Format.)

The result is an exceptionally modern-style report—clear, concise, and throughly fascinating. *The Mayflower Report, 1622* is indeed the story that made America.

---

1 However, this edition retains Old Style dates, even though the Gregorian calendar later shifted all dates forward by ten days. The archaic dates, though, do not change the narrative. The Pilgrims *believed* their dates were correct and acted accordingly, e.g., celebrating Christmas on their December 25, 1620, even though the date was later officially corrected to January 4, 1621.

New Format

For centuries, Americans have repeatedly restored the original Pilgrim travelogue, *Mourt's Relation,*[1] into a more readable form. *The Mayflower Report, 1622* is the restoration for our era.

Nevertheless, the process of restoration is inherently subjective, i.e., a matter of opinion. Hazy passages and odd grammar are clarified in light of modern scholarship, but certainty is impossible—most places in America had no English names when the Pilgrims arrived, making their exact itinerary difficult to confirm.

This book is also a changed and annotated text with more concise sentences and paragraphs; it is *not* a verbatim reprint. It strives to recover the meaning of the saga, rather than its exact wording. However, this edition retains some historic spellings and grammar; these archaic forms may reflect secondary meanings, emotional tone, linguistic variations, quaint phrasing, etc.

Several additional methods annotate and explain the narrative. Antiquated phrases or words, including native names, are *italicized*; possible modern equivalents, including place-names and new chapter subheadings, are in *[bracketed italics]*; ambiguous passages are clarified via "best guess" in [bracketed plain-text]; and editor's notes provide background history in **[bracketed boldface]**.

Illustrations are mostly nineteenth-century interpretations. Some scenes are based on early Indian life in Virginia and the Carolinas; these images may have been known to the Pilgrims before their arrival in America.

However, the only image of a Pilgrim based on an actual portrait is that of Edward Winslow, one of the Pilgrim authors (see page 17).[2] No confirmed portraits exist for other Pilgrims—their images are only artistic interpretations. Hence, in many ways, the Mayflower Pilgrims remain elusive legends, which perhaps is what they intended.

---

1 William Bradford and Edward Winslow, *et al., A Relation or Journall* [sic] *of the beginning and proceedings of the English Plantation setled* [sic] *at Plimoth in New England* (London: John Bellamie, 1622).

2 The inverted image on page 17 depicts Edward Winslow at age 24 in July 1620. However, the artist, Robert Weir, painted it in 1843, based on a true-life portrait done in 1651, when Mr. Winslow was 55.

New Note about Original Prefaces

The original report by the Mayflower Pilgrims began with three prefaces by three different friends of theirs— Robert Cushman, George Morton,[1] and John Robinson, the Pilgrim minister. However, none of the three sailed aboard the *Mayflower,* and none wrote the main report.

Not surprisingly, their prefaces offer little information about the Pilgrims' experience in America. Rather, the prefaces were written separately, regarding other matters occurring *before* or *after* the main narrative.[2]

Accordingly, the original prefaces appear only as appendices at the end of this book. Instead, the revised narrative opens with the Pilgrims describing their own departure from England for America aboard the tall-masted ship *Mayflower*.

Their vessel heads west across the Atlantic Ocean and quickly disappears over the horizon. Fierce storms soon follow. Many months pass without word from the Pilgrims. Their friends and family fear that the colonists have perished, joining other doomed expeditions of the era.

Yet suddenly, there is electrifying news: The Pilgrims are alive! And there is more—they report one of the greatest and most hopeful adventures in human history.

That momentous first report now follows. From across the centuries, the Pilgrims speak to us once more ...

---

1 George Morton's authorship is speculative. See Appendix D.
2 Of the three prefaces, Rev. Robinson's has the most historical value, being a sermon delivered to the Pilgrims just before they departed for America. His passing reference to "strangers" has sometimes been misinterpreted as dismissive of outsiders. The sermon itself, though, makes it clear that Rev. Robinson advises tolerance and generosity of spirit to *all* people.

[Original Title & Contents Page]

A
RELATION OR
Journal of the Beginning and Proceedings

of the English Plantation settled at Plymouth[1] in
NEW ENGLAND by certain English Adventurers,
both Merchants and others.[2]

With their difficult passage, their safe arrival, their
joyful building of, and comfortable planting themselves
in the now well-defended Town
of New Plymouth.

AS ALSO A RELATION OF FOUR [Episodes]
[with] several discoveries since made by some of the
same English Planters there resident **[in original italics directly below]**:

I. In a journey to Pokanoket[3] [an Indian kingdom in Rhode Island], *[the colonists visit] the habitation of the Indians' greatest king,* Massasoit. *[Herein is], as also, their message; [and] the answer and entertainment they had of him.*
II. In a voyage made by ten of them to the Kingdom of Nauset [Indian territory on Cape Cod], *[the colonists go] to seek a boy that had lost himself in the woods; with such accidents as befall them in that voyage.*
III. In their journey to the Kingdom of Nemasket[4] [near present-day Middleborough, Massachusetts], *[the colonists fight] in defense of their greatest king,* Massasoit, *against the* Narrohiggonsets [the Narragansett Indians]; *and to revenge the supposed death of their interpreter,* Tisquantum.
IIII. [In] their voyage to the Massachusetts [an Indian tribe at Boston Bay] *and their entertainment there, [the colonists negotiate peace].*

With an answer to all such objections as are, in any way,
made against the lawfulness of English plantations
in those parts.

---

1   *Plymouth* replaces the ancient spellings, *Plimoth, Plimmoth,* or *Plimmouth.*
2   The "merchants" remained in England; the "others" went to America.
3   *Pokanoket* replaces a 1622 spelling, *Puckanokick.*
4   The modernized *Nemasket* replaces the original *Namaschet.*

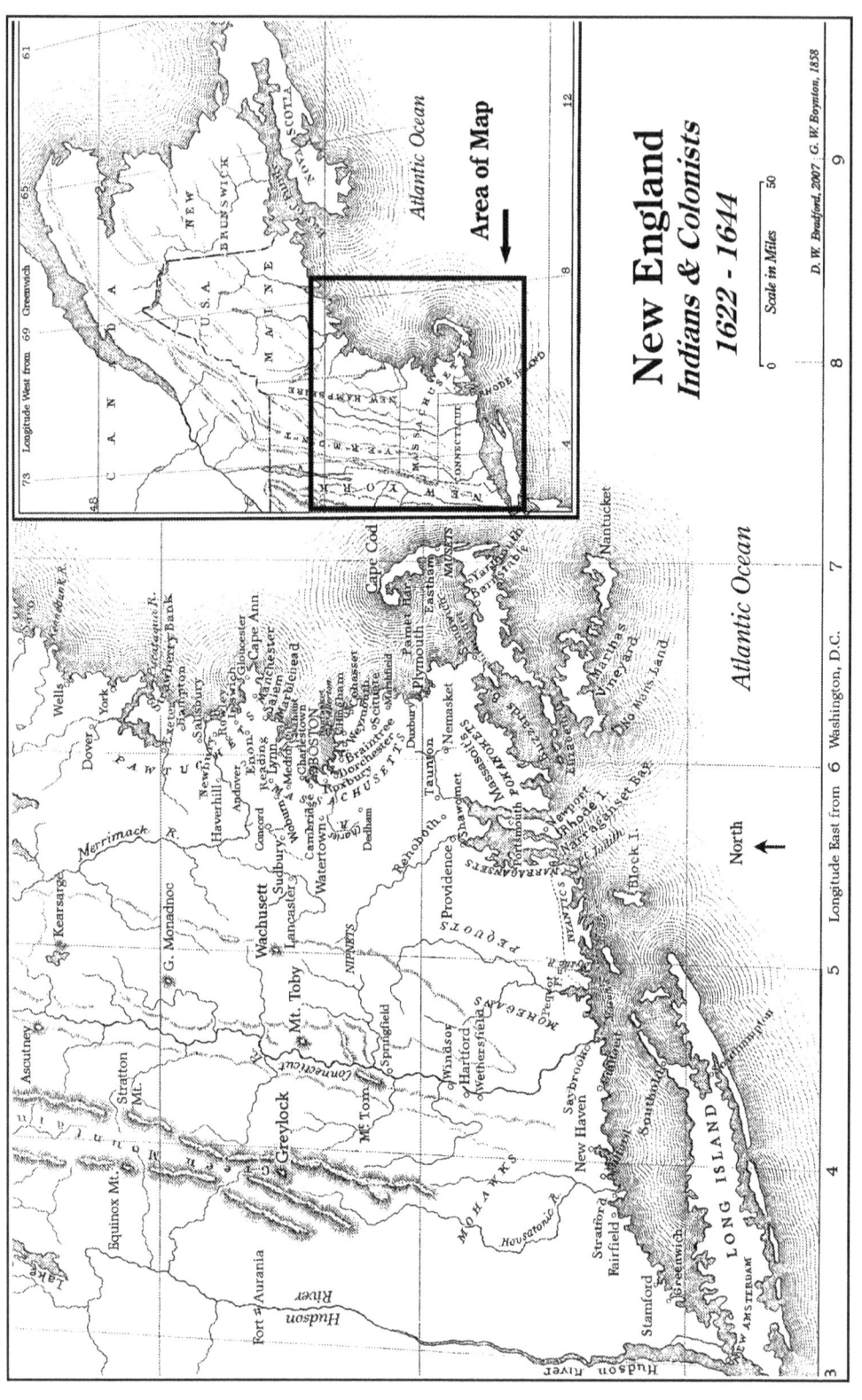

[The Main Report]

A RELATION OR
JOURNAL OF THE
PROCEEDINGS OF THE
Plantation Settled at [New] Plymouth in New England
[with modern annotation in italics and/or brackets].

*[Departure from England,
and Arrival in America]*

Wednesday, the 6th of September [1620] – The wind [was] coming east-northeast—a fine, small gale. We loosed [our ship's moorings] from Plymouth [England], having been kindly entertained and *courteously used [warmly hosted as guests]* by diverse friends there dwelling. [The sailing ship *Mayflower* headed west for America, requiring over two months to cross the Atlantic Ocean.]

And after many difficulties in boisterous storms, at length by God's Providence upon the 9th of November following, by break of the day [at sunrise], we *espied*[1] land which we deemed to be Cape Cod—and so afterward it proved.

And the appearance of it much comforted us, especially seeing so goodly a land, and wooded [with many trees] to the brink of the sea. It caused us to rejoice together and praise God that had given us once again to see land.

---

1 Past tense of the medieval word, *espy,* i.e., to see something from afar.

Engraving of John Smith's Map of New England, Circa 1614 Cape Cod is noted as "Cape James" at lower left.

[Anchorage at Cape Cod]

And thus we made our course south-southwest, purposing [or intending] to go to a river *[the present-day Hudson River]*, ten leagues *[thirty miles]* to the south of the Cape.[1] But at night, the wind being contrary, we put round again for the Bay of Cape Cod.

And [the next day], upon the 11th of November [1620], we came to an anchor[age] in the bay *[at Provincetown Harbor, Massachusetts]*, which is a good harbor and pleasant bay. [Its shape is] circled-round —except in the entrance, which is about four miles over from land to land—compassed about to the very sea with [many kinds of trees]: oaks, pines, juniper, sassafras, and other sweet wood. It is a harbor wherein 1,000 sail of ships may safely ride.

There we relieved ourselves with [fresh supplies]—[fire]wood and water—and refreshed our people, while our *shallop [a sailboat]* was fitted to coast the bay to search for an habitation [a place to live].

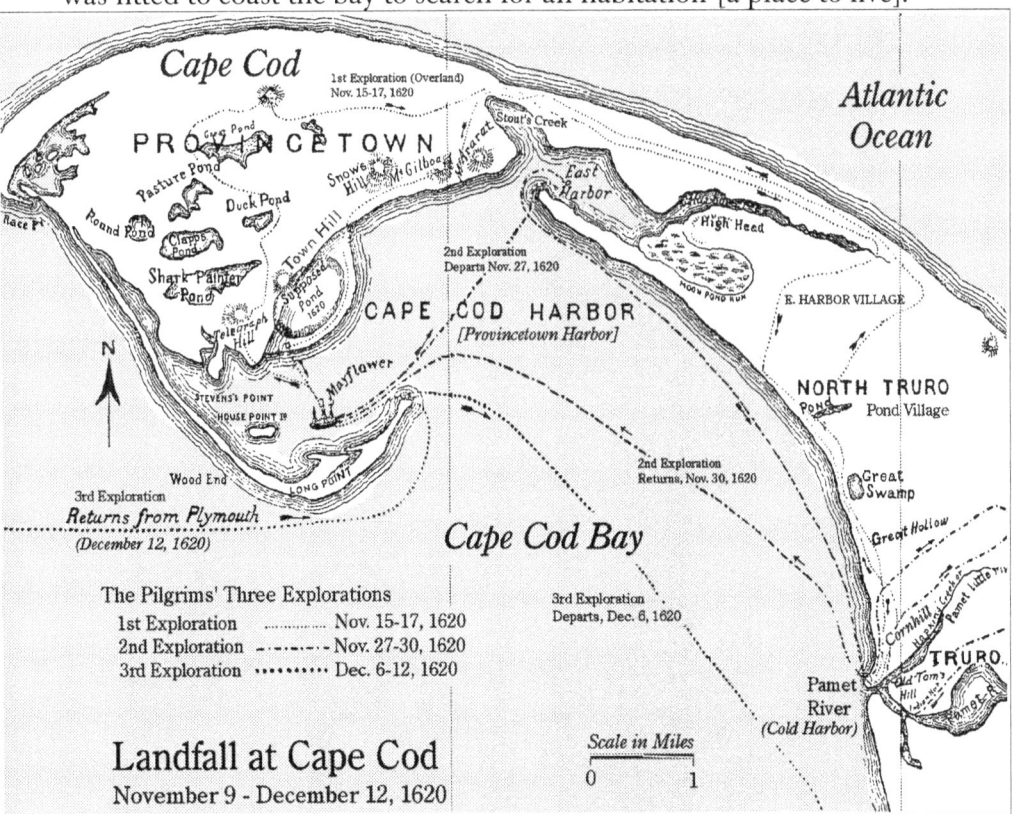

___
1 The Pilgrims erred about the Hudson River; it was 200, not 30, miles away.

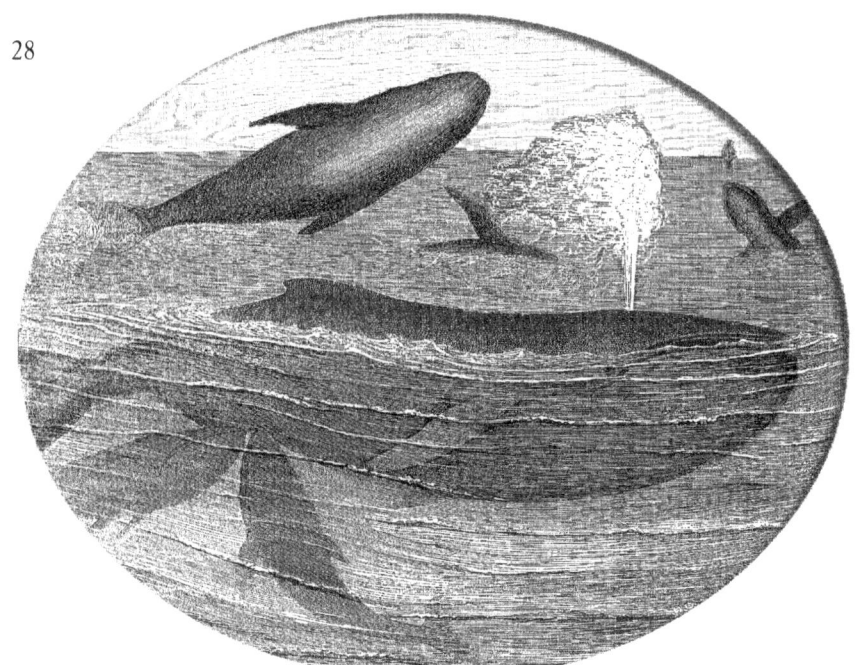

[Whales at Play]

[At Cape Cod] there was the greatest store of fowl [the most and fattest game birds for feasting] that ever we saw. And everyday, we saw whales playing hard-by us [breaching the water near the ship].

[Concerning whales] of which in that place, if we had instruments and means to take them [as a fishing catch], we might have made a very rich return, which, to our great grief, we wanted. Our Master [the *Mayflower's* captain] and his Mate [the second-in-command] and others experienced in fishing professed we might have made three or four thousand pounds worth of oil [from catching whales]. They preferred it before Greenland whale-fishing and purpose [or plan] the next winter to fish for whale here.

"Fishing" for Whales in Greenland

[Poor Fishing]

For cod, we assayed [by fishing in the harbor near the anchored *Mayflower*], but found none. [The best times for codfish are spring and summer]; there is good store, no doubt, in their season.

Neither got we any fish [of other kinds], all the time we lay there, but some few little ones on the shore. We found great mussels—and very fat and full of sea pearl—but we could not eat them. For they made us all sick, [those] that did eat, [afflicting] as well sailors as passengers. They caused [many of us] to *cast and scour [vomit and have diarrhea]*, but they were soon well again.

Fishing for Cod

The bay *[at Provincetown Harbor]* is so round and circling that before we could come to anchor, we went round all the points of the compass. We [aboard the *Mayflower*] could not come near the shore by three quarters of an English mile because of shallow water *[filled with submerged drifts of sand called "flat sands" or tidal flats]*, which was a great prejudice to us. For our people going on-shore were forced to wade a *bow shoot or two*[1] in going a-land [after rowing small boats part way to the beach, and disembarking in water above the knees for 60 to 140 yards], which caused many to get colds and coughs. For it was nigh-times[2] freezing-cold weather.

---

1 *Bow shoot* is either the *bow*-to-stern length of a ship (about thirty yards), or a minimum range of an arrow shot from a simple *bow* (seventy yards).
2 Misprinted in 1622 as *ny times.* Another interpretation is *many times.*

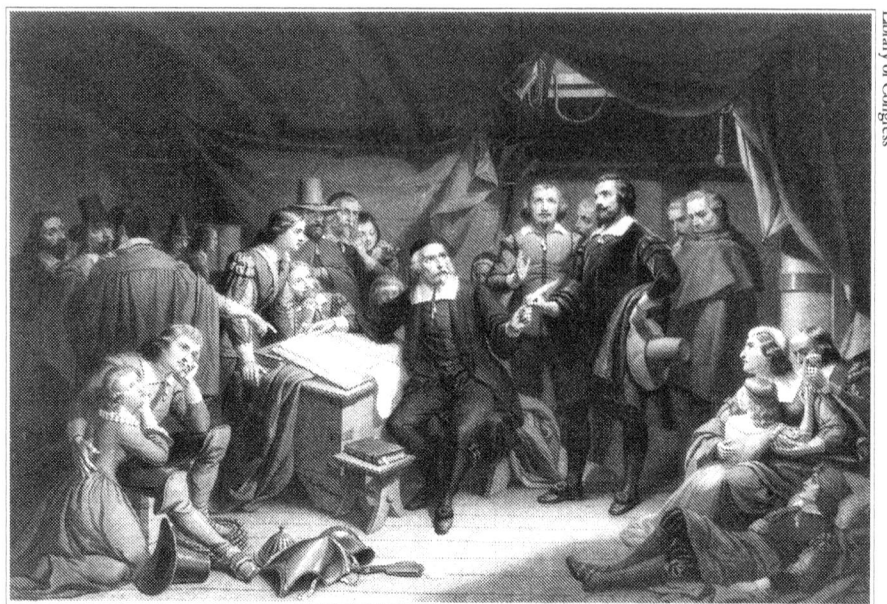

[New Government]

This day [11th of November 1620], before we came to harbor, [we had been] observing some [of our passengers] not well affected to unite and concord, but gave some appearance of *faction [infighting]*. It was thought good [that] there should be an association and agreement—that we should combine together in one body and to submit to such government and governors as we should, by common consent, agree to make and choose. And [we] set our hands to this, [signing the agreement] that follows, word-for-word:

[The Mayflower Compact][1]

In the name of God, Amen. We—whose names are underwritten, the loyal subjects of our dread sovereign, Lord King JAMES, by the grace of God, of Great Britain, France, and Ireland, King, Defender of the Faith, etc.—having undertaken for the glory of God, and advancement of the Christian Faith, and honor of our King and Country, a voyage to plant the first Colony in the Northern parts of Virginia,[2] do, *by these presents [by these legal*

---

1 The Mayflower Compact established an early representative government in America; minor changes in punctuation have been made here.
2 The Pilgrims had intended to settle the Hudson River Valley in New York, then part of northern Virginia. They landed inadvertently in Massachusetts.

writings], solemnly and mutually in the presence of God and one of another, covenant and combine ourselves together into a civil body politic for our better ordering and preservation and furtherance of the ends aforesaid; and by virtue hereof, to enact, constitute, and frame such just and equal laws, ordinances, acts, constitutions [and][1] offices from time to time as shall be thought most *meet [appropriate]* and convenient for the general good of the Colony, unto which we promise all due submission and obedience. In witness whereof, we have hereunder subscribed our names,

>Cape Cod
>11th of November in the year of the reign of our sovereign
>   Lord King JAMES, of England, France, and
>Ireland, 18 [years of reign]; and of Scotland, 54 [years].
>*Anno Domini [in the year of the Lord]* 1620.

[Going Ashore][2]

The same day [the 11th of November 1620], so soon as we could, we set ashore fifteen or sixteen men, well-armed *[at Stevens Point at the western end of present-day Provincetown, Massachusetts on Cape Cod]*. [The men went as guards] with some [of our other people] to fetch [fire]wood, for we had none left. [We hoped] as also to see what the land was [at the tip of Cape Cod], and what inhabitants they could meet with.

They found it to be a small neck of land [with water on two sides]. On this side where we lay is the bay *[Provincetown Harbor]*; and [on] the further side, the sea [the Atlantic Ocean].

The ground or earth [is often covered with] sand hills, much like the *downes [the coastal sand dunes]* in Holland, but much better. The crust of the earth [is] a spit's depth—excellent black earth [a shovelful deep]. All [is] wooded with oaks, pines, sassafras, juniper, birch, holly, vines, some ash, walnut. The wood[s], for the most part, [are] open and without underwood, fit either to go or ride in [being passable either on foot or on horseback].

---

1 William Bradford, a Pilgrim author, inserted the "[and]" at a later date. The other annotation to the Mayflower Compact is modern to this edition.

2 Also on November 11, 1620, the Pilgrims elected John Carver to be their first governor in America. However, worried about a hostile English king, they buried their governor's identity toward the back of the book (see page 95).

At night, our people returned [from exploring the area around the tip of Cape Cod] but found not any person nor habitation. And [our people had] laded their boat with juniper, which smelled very sweet and strong, and of which we burnt [for firewood] the most part of the time we lay there.

Monday, the 13th of November [1620] – We unshipped our shallop [unpacking a large sailboat stored aboard the *Mayflower*] and

drew her on land to mend and repair her, having been forced to cut her down in bestowing her betwixt the decks.[1]

And she was much opened [with many small leaks], with the peoples lying in her [as an open sleeping area during the long voyage to America. Repairs on the shallop, or sailboat, were slow] which kept us long there. For it was sixteen or seventeen days, before the carpenter had finished her.[2]

[Wash & Explore]

[Also on Monday, the 13th of November], our people went on shore *[south of Town Hill in present-day Provincetown]* to refresh themselves—and our women to wash [clothes],[3] as they had great

---

1 The Pilgrims' *shallop*, or sailboat, could roam coastal waters that were too shallow for the deep hull of the *Mayflower*. The nimble *shallop*, though, could still carry dozens of men and sail rough seas as far away as Maine.
2 John Alden, a crew member of the *Mayflower* and a specialist in making water-tight barrels, likely assisted the ship's carpenter with repairs to the sailboat. The poet Henry Longfellow later claimed Mr. Alden, age 21, fell in love with a young woman among the Pilgrims and stayed in America to court her. Mr. Longfellow told the story in his bestselling epic, *The Courtship of Miles Standish*, since restored as *The Romance of Pilgrims* by Boston Hill Press. (Captain Standish was allegedly the third member of a Pilgrim love-triangle.)
3 Possibly at a small pond near the shore, since eroded away by storm surges.

need. But [most men were idle] whilst we lay thus still, hoping our shallop would be ready in five or six days, at the furthest. But our carpenter made slow work of it.

[Winter approached] so that some of our people, impatient of delay, desired [to search for a place to build our new town] for our better furtherance. [They wanted] to *travail*[1] by land [or go on foot] into the country, which was not without appearance of danger.

Not having the shallop with them, nor means to carry provision but on their backs, [they wanted to explore the area] to see whether it might be fit for us to seat in or no [as a place to live]. And the rather, [they sought a waterway] because as we sailed into the harbor, there seemed to be a river opening itself into the mainland.

The willingness of the persons [to explore] was liked, but the thing itself [walking into the wilderness by themselves], in regard of the danger, was rather permitted than[2] approved.

And so, with [Governor John Carver giving] cautions, directions, and instructions, sixteen men were set out, with every man his musket [or long-barreled gun], sword, and *corselet [steel body-armor]*. [They were] under the conduct of Captain Miles Standish, unto whom was adjoined for counsel and advice, William Bradford, Stephen Hopkins, and Edward Tilley.

[Editor's Note: This exploration party included two of the most famous Pilgrims, Miles Standish, their military advisor, and William Bradford, an author of this report and future governor of the colony. They had an unusual relationship on this first exploration of Cape Cod—the Pilgrims placed the lower-ranked Miles Standish in command, with William Bradford, his political superior, under him.

This inverted hierarchy was rare in an era of feudal privilege. However, the Pilgrims had a religiously-inspired vision of public service—a man's rank reflected only his ability to serve God and society. Miles Standish, a professional soldier, could better help the Pilgrims on a hazardous expedition and hence earned temporary command over William Bradford, then already a deputy governor.

This merger of religion and practicality served the Pilgrims well. Their unique values created a new, democratic society in America, one very different from the class-bound England they left behind.]

---

1 In the post-medieval era, *travel* required *travail*, i.e., great effort.
2 The 1622 text often uses *then* for *than*. This edition corrects such instances.

[The First Exploration]

Wednesday, the 15th of November [1620] – They [our first explorers] were set ashore *[near present-day Telegraph Hill at the western end of Provincetown on Cape Cod]*. [See map, page 27.]

And when they had ordered themselves in the order of a single file and marched about the space of a mile by the sea[1] *[to near the west side of Town Hill]*,[2] they espied five or six people, with a dog, coming towards them.[3] [They were Indians] who were savages—who, when they saw them [our explorers], ran into the wood[s] and whistled the dog after them, etc.

[Our men initially did not believe them to be Indians.] First, they supposed them to be Master Jones, the Master [or captain of the *Mayflower*],[4] and some of his men. For they were ashore and knew of their coming. But after they knew them to be Indians, they marched after them into the woods *[near a small body of water later called Duck Pond]*, lest other of the Indians should lie in ambush.

But when the Indians saw our men following them, they ran away with might and main. And our men turned out of the wood[s] after them [going ahead to block their escape], for it was the way they intended to go. But they could not come near them.

---

1 Clause incorporates changes made later by William Bradford. The 1622 text is more ambiguous about the relative positions of Pilgrims and Indians.
2 Also dubbed High Hill, but Town Hill seems intended. Justin Winsor, 8 vol. *Narrative & Critical History of America* (Boston: Houghton Mifflin, 1884) 3:270.
3 Another interpretation could be "...they espied five or six people, *with a dog coming towards them who were savages,*" i.e., the dog approaches *the Indians*.
4 The *Master* of a ship was its commanding officer, i.e., the captain of the ship.

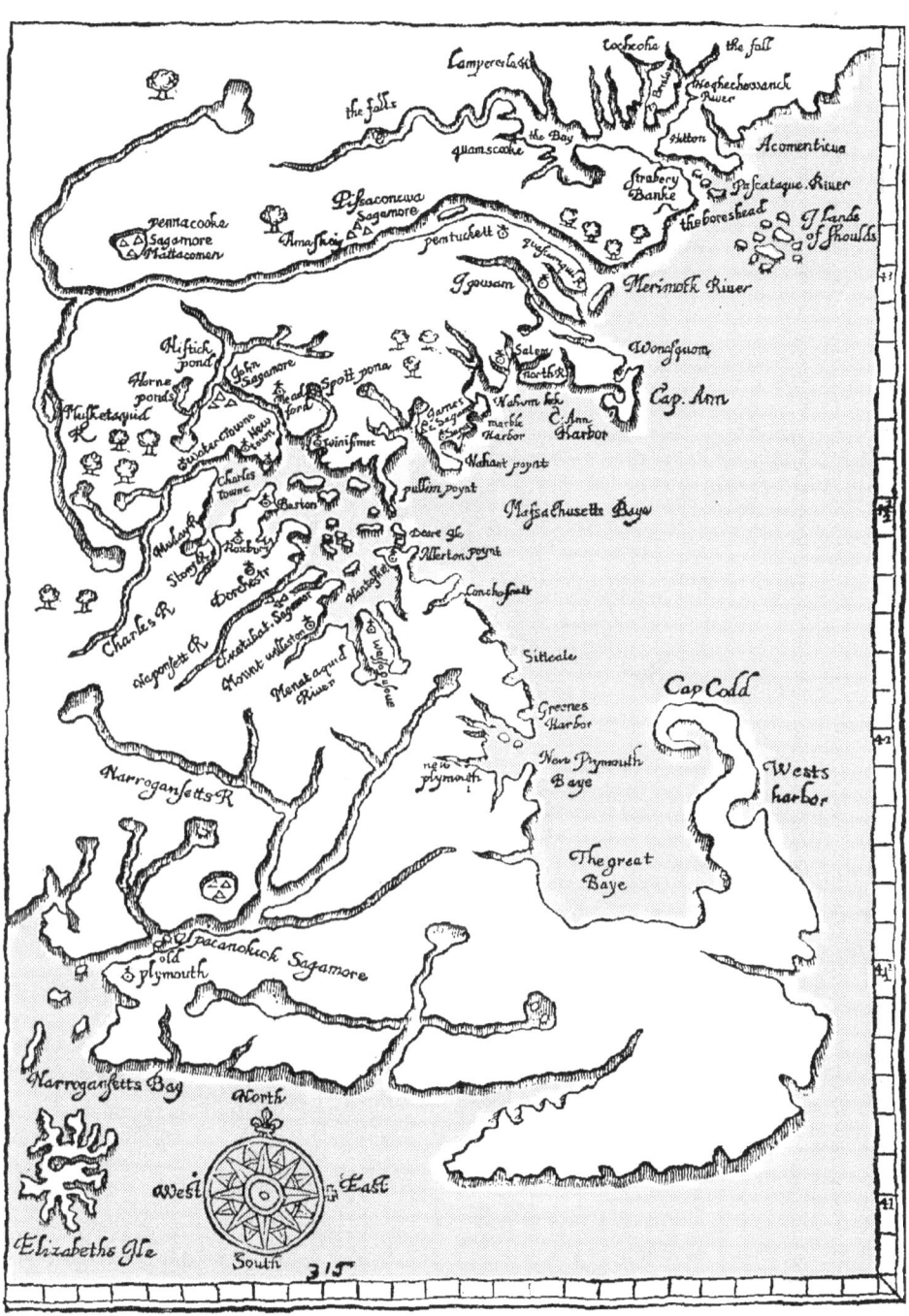

Map of Southern New England in 1634

[The First Camp]

[All that day and after sunset, the explorers pursued the Indians.] They followed them that night about ten miles by the trace of their footings and saw how they had come the same way they went. And, at a turning, [our men] perceived how they run up an hill *[near a peak called Oak Head]* to see whether they followed them.

At length, night came upon them, and they [the explorers] were  constrained to take up their lodging *[near Stout's Creek, since engulfed by Pilgrim Lake, not far from the Atlantic seacoast]*. So, they set forth three sentinels, and the rest [of the group made camp]—some kindled a fire, and others fetched wood. And there [we] held our rendezvous [or first campsite] that night.

[Thursday, the 16th of November 1620] – In the morning, so soon as we could see the trace [of the Indians' footsteps], we proceeded on our journey and had the track [heading southeast near the Atlantic seacoast] until we had compassed the head of a long creek— *[passed the headwaters of East Harbor Creek, now a wetland called Head of the Meadow in Cape Cod National Seashore]*.

And there, they [the Indians] took into another wood *[turning into a forest near present-day Pilgrim Heights]*, and we [went] after them, supposing to find some of their dwellings. But we marched through boughs and bushes, and under hills and valleys, which tore our very armor in pieces.[1]

And yet, [we] could meet with none of them nor their houses, nor find any fresh water, which we greatly desired and stood in need of. For we brought neither beer nor water with us. And our victuals[2] was only biscuit and Holland cheese—and a little bottle of *aqua vitae [alcoholic liquor]*, so as we were sore a-thirst.

---

1   Damage to intricate links of chain mail or to leather fasteners of steel plates.
2   Pronounced as *vittles,* the modern slang for food.

About ten o'clock[1] [in the morning], we came into a deep valley full of brush, *wood-gale [bayberry plants[2]]* and long grass through which we found little paths or tracks.

And there we saw a deer and found springs of fresh water *[in a place now called Pilgrim Spring]*, of which we were heartily glad and sat us down and drunk our first New England water—with as much delight as ever we *drunk drink*[3] in all our lives .

When we had refreshed ourselves, we directed our course full South [so] that we might come to the shore [of the Bay of Cape Cod], which, within a short while after, we did. And there [we] made a fire [so] that they in the ship might see where we were, as we had direction [from Governor Carver to signal that we were safe].

And so [we] marched on towards this supposed river. And as we went in another valley, we found a fine, clear pond of fresh water, being about a musket-shot broad [or one-hundred yards wide] and twice as long *[at Pond Village, now in North Truro, Massachusetts]*. There grew also many small vines, and fowl and deer haunted there. There [also] grew much sassafras [a medicinal tree].[4]

From thence, we went on and found much plain ground, about fifty acres fit for the plow, and some signs where the Indians had formerly planted their corn. After this, some thought it best for [finding the] nearness of the river to go down [to the shore of the bay] and travail on the sea sands—[plod through the sand dunes along the beach]—by which means, some of our men were tired and lagged behind. So we stayed and gathered them up.

---

1 *O'clock* is a modernized spelling; the 1622 text uses *a clocke*.
2 An aromatic shrub, whose leaves produced wax for candles.
3 Either quaint phrasing or a possible misprint from 1622.
4 Sassafras trees yielded folk medicines and root beer. The Pilgrims later harvested the bark and roots for shipment to England as a cash crop.

[Tombs]

And [we] struck into the land again, where we found a little path to certain heaps of sand. One whereof was covered with old mats and had a wooden thing like a *mortar whelmed [an upside-down bowl]* on the top of it. And an earthen pot laid in a little hole at the end [of the heap of sand] thereof.

We, musing what it might be, digged and found a bow and, as we thought, arrows—but they were rotten.

We supposed there were many other things [buried in the heaps], but because we deemed them graves, we put in the bow again [reburying it in the sand] and made it up as it was. And [we] left the rest untouched because we thought it would be odious unto them to ransack their sepulchers.

We went on further and found new stubble [of harvested cornstalks], of which they had gotten corn this year. And [there were] many walnut trees full of nuts and great store of strawberries and some vines.

Passing thus a field or two, which were not great, we came to another which had also been new gotten [or freshly harvested]. And there we found where an house had been, and four or five old planks laid together. Also, we found a great kettle which had been some ship's kettle and brought out of Europe.[1]

There was also an heap of sand, made like the former, but it was newly done [with finger marks]; we might see how they had paddled it with their hands. [We examined the heap], which we digged up. And in it, we found a little old basket full of fair Indian corn.

---

1   A French ship ran aground a few years before the Pilgrims arrived.

And [we] digged further and found a fine, great new basket. [It was] full of very fair corn of this year, with some thirty-six goodly ears of corn—some yellow and some red and others mixed with blue—which was a very goodly sight.

The basket was round and narrow at the top. It held about three or four bushels, which was as much as two of us could lift up from the ground. And [the basket] was very handsomely and cunningly made.

[Survival versus Honesty]

But whilst we were busy about these things, we set our men [as] sentinel in a round ring [of defense]. [Every man stood guard], all but two or three which digged up the corn.

We were in suspense what to do with it [the corn] and the kettle. [We did not want to steal, but had great need.] And, at length, after much consultation, we concluded to take the kettle and as much of the corn as we could carry away with us.

And [we decided that] when our shallop came [to this location again]—if we could find any of the [Indian] people and come to parley with them—we would give them the kettle again and satisfy them for their corn [making complete repayment].

So we took all the ears [of corn] and put a good deal of the loose corn in the kettle for two men to bring away on a staff.[1] Besides, they that could put any into their pockets, filled the same. The rest [of the corn] we buried again—for we were so laden with armor, that we could carry no more.

[Editor's Note: The Pilgrims were short of food and seed due to their untimely arrival in a frozen wilderness. Yet, their religious and moral values made them averse to stealing, even though honesty might mean starvation. Moreover, the Pilgrims were not just posturing for future historians. The Pilgrims *did* later find the owners of the corn and *did* repay them. The Pilgrims kept their word, not just to the absent Indians, but to a God whom the Pilgrims believed sees and judges all.]

---

1 The Pilgrims dangled the kettle from the staff and lifted the two ends.

[The Fort at the Pamet River]

Not far from this place [of Indian corn], we found the remainder of an old fort or palisade which, as we conceived, had been made by some Christians. This was also hard-by that place [near a waterway flowing into the Bay of Cape Cod] which we thought had been a river, unto which we went. And [we] found it so to be [a great river], dividing itself into two arms by an high bank *[later named Old Tom's Hill in present-day Truro, Massachusetts]* standing right by the cut or mouth which came from the sea.

That [branch of the river] which was next unto us *[Hopkin's Creek or present-day Pamet Little River]* was the less [in width]. The other arm *[the Pamet River]* was more than twice as big and not unlike[ly] to be an harbor for ships. [See map, page 27.] But whether it be a fresh river or only an indraft of the sea, we had no time to discover. For we had commandment [from Governor Carver] to be out [from the *Mayflower*] but two days.

Here also, we saw two canoes, the one on the one side, the other on the other side *[of Pamet Little River]*. We could not believe it was a canoe, till we came near it.

So we returned [the same way we came], leaving the further discovery [of the waterways] hereof to our shallop. And [we] came that night back again to the freshwater pond.

[Night Watch]

And there we made our rendezvous [or camp] that night. [Finding the canoes made us fear for Indians], we making a great fire and *a barricado [a wall of tree branches]* to windward of us. And [we] kept good watch with three sentinels all night, everyone standing when his turn came, while five or six inches of *match [a slow gun-fuse]* was burning [ready to fire our guns].[1]

---
1 Their *match-lock* guns required a pre-lit fuse or *match* to ignite gunpowder.

It proved a very rainy night. In the morning [of Friday, the 17th of November], we took our kettle and sunk it in the pond [planning to retrieve it later]—and trimmed our muskets,[1] for few of them would go off because of the wet. And so [we] coasted the wood, [hiking through the forest] again to come home. [But the trees were so thick] in which we were shrewdly puzzled and lost our way.

As we wandered [northeast across Cape Cod to the Atlantic coast], we came to a tree where a young sprit [or sapling] was bowed down over a bow and some acorns strewed underneath. Stephen Hopkins said it had been [made by the Indians] to catch some deer.

So, as we were looking at it, William Bradford, being in the rear when he came, looked also upon it. And as he went about, it gave a sudden jerk up, and he was immediately caught by the leg.

It was a very pretty device made [by Indians] with a rope of their own making and having a noose as artificially made as any roper in England can make and as like [ropes of] ours as can be. [We much admired the rope], which we brought away with us.

In the end, we got out of the wood[s] [at the wrong place] and were fallen about a mile too high above the creek *[emerging upstream of the headwaters of East Harbor Creek,[2] near present-day Head-of-the-Meadow Beach on the Atlantic seacoast]* where we saw three [deer] bucks. [In our haste, we left them alone], but we had rather have had one of them [to eat].

---

1 *Muskets* were guns resembling modern rifles but had exposed parts. Rain dampened their gunpowder, necessitating cleaning and drying.
2 The creek is now a wetland or "salt meadow" in Cape Cod National Seashore.

Partridge

We also did spring three couple of partridges [into the air]. And, as we came along by the creek, we saw great flocks of wild geese and ducks, but they were very fearful of us.

So we marched some while in the woods, some while on the sands, and otherwhile in the water up to the knees, till at length we came *[back to the shore of Provincetown, south of Town Hill]* near the ship.

And then we shot off our [gun]-pieces, and the longboat [a rowboat] came [from the *Mayflower*] to fetch us. Master Jones [the ship's captain] and Master[1] Carver [our governor], being on the shore with many of our people, came to meet us. And thus, we came both weary and welcome home—and delivered in our corn into the store[room] to be kept for seed.

Canada Goose

For we knew not how to come by any [more corn]. And therefore [we] were very glad [to have found Indian supplies], purposing—so soon as we could meet with any of the inhabitants of that place—to make them large satisfaction [by repaying them for the corn]. (This[2] was our first [journey of] discovery whilst our shallop [or sailboat] was in repairing.)

[Cold and Wet]

Our people did make things as fitting as they could and time would [permit] in seeking out wood and *helving of tools [making wood-handles for axes and saws]* and sawing of timber to build a new shallop. But the discommodiousness of the harbor [or its shallow depth] did much hinder us. For we could neither go to, nor come from the shore [to ferry supplies from the *Mayflower*] but at high [tide]water, which was much to our hindrance and hurt.

For oftentimes, they [our people] waded to the middle of the thigh and oft to the knees to go and come from land. Some did it necessarily, and some for their own pleasure, but it brought to the

---

1 *Master* is a title here, equivalent to *Mr.* for *Mister*.
2 Possible misprint; the text could also be "*Thus* was our first discovery ..."

most, if not to all, coughs and colds. The weather [was] proving suddenly cold and stormy, which afterward turned [people] to the scurvy, whereof many died.¹

[The Second Exploration]

[Monday, 27th of November 1620] – When our shallop was fit [to float, but] indeed, before she was fully fitted—for there was two-days work after[wards] bestowed on her—there was appointed some twenty-four men of our own, and [we] armed them² to go and make a more full discovery of the rivers before mentioned.

Master Jones [the *Mayflower's* captain] was desirous to go with us and took [with him] such of his sailors as he thought useful for us. So, as we were [a large group]—in all about thirty-four men—we made Master Jones our leader [on this exploration]. For we thought it best herein to gratify his kindness and forwardness.

[We planned to sail south along the shore of Cape Cod, but] when we were set forth, it proved rough weather and cross winds. So, as we were constrained, some [of us] in the shallop and others in the longboat [had] to row to the nearest shore [that] the wind would suffer them to go unto. And then [all had] to wade out [in water] above the knees *[onto Beach Point at the mouth of East Harbor, since diked to form Pilgrim Lake]*. [See map, page 27.]

The wind was so strong as the shallop could not keep [to] the water [of the bay], but was forced to harbor there that night *[in East Harbor]*. But we [left the boats and] marched six or seven miles further [south along the shore] and appointed the shallop, [asking the crew] to come to us as soon as they could. It blowed and did snow all that day and night—and froze withal. Some of our people that are dead took the original [cause] of their death here.

---

1   Scurvy is a debilitating disease caused by malnutrition. However, the Pilgrims seem here to conflate scurvy with influenza; the Pilgrims suffered from both.
2   The 1622 text is "and armed, *then* to go," probably a misprint.

The next day [Tuesday, the 28th of November 1620], about eleven o'clock, our shallop came to us *[from East Harbor]*, and we shipped ourselves. And the wind being good, we sailed [south] to the river we formerly discovered, which we named *Cold Harbor [now called the Pamet River]*—to which when we came, we found it not navigable for [large] ships. Yet, we thought it might be a good harbor for [small] boats, for it flows there twelve foot at high water.

We landed our men *[at Old Tom's Hill in present-day Truro, Massachusetts]* between the two creeks *[Pamet River and Pamet Little River]* and marched some four or five miles by the greater of them *[the Pamet]*. And [entering the river] the shallop followed us.

At length, night grew on, and our men were tired with marching up and down the steep hills and deep valleys which lay half a foot thick with snow. Master Jones [the *Mayflower's* captain], wearied with marching, was desirous we should take up our lodging—though some of us would have marched further.

So we made there our rendezvous [or camp] for that night, under a few pine trees. And, as it fell out, we [went hunting with our guns and] got three fat geese and six ducks to our supper—which we eat with soldiers' stomachs, for we had eaten little all that day.

Our resolution was next morning to go up to the head of this river, for we supposed it would prove fresh water. But in the morning, our resolution held not because many liked not the hilliness of the soil and badness of the harbor.

So we turned [north] towards the other creek *[Pamet Little River]* [so] that we might go over and look for the rest of the corn that we left behind when we were here before. When we came to the creek, we saw the canoe

Brent Goose

lie on the dry ground, and a flock of geese in the river, at which one [of us] made a shot and killed a couple of them. And we launched the canoe and fetched them.

[Return to Corn Hill]

And when we had done [fetching the geese with the canoe], she carried us over [the creek] by seven or eight at once. This done, we marched to the place where we had [found] the corn formerly, which place we called Corn Hill. And [we] digged and found the rest [of the corn], of which we were very glad.

We also digged in a place a little further off and found a bottle of oil. We went to another place which we had seen before and digged—and [we] found more corn, *viz.,* two or three baskets full of Indian wheat, and a bag of beans with a good many of fair wheat-ears [of corn].[1]

Whilst some of us were digging up this, some others found another heap of corn, which they digged up also, so as we had in all about ten bushels—which will serve us sufficiently for seed.

| Note. | And sure it was God's good providence that we found this corn,[2] for else we know not how we should have done [to obtain seed]. For we knew not how we should find or meet with any of the Indians [to trade for corn], except it be to do us a mischief.

Also, we had never in all likelihood seen a grain of it, if we had not made our first journey [to discover this area of Cape Cod]. For

---

1   Indian "wheat" is corn or *maize*, related to modern "corn on the cob."
2   All margin notes are from the original text.

the ground was now covered with snow and so hard frozen that we were *fain [required]* with our *curtlaxes [hand axes]* and short swords to hew and carve the ground a foot deep—and then wrest it up with levers—for we had forgot to bring other tools.

Whilst we were in this employment, foul weather [was] being towards [as a storm approached]. Master Jones [the *Mayflower's* captain] was earnest to go aboard [to safeguard his ship], but sundry of us desired to make further discovery and to find out the Indians' habitations. So we sent home with him our weakest people—and some that were sick—and all the corn.

And eighteen of us stayed still and lodged there that night. And [we] desired that the shallop might return to us next day and bring us some *mattocks [picks]* and spades with them.

The next morning we followed certain beaten paths and tracks of the Indians into the woods, supposing they would have led us into some town or houses. After we had gone a while, we light upon a very broad, beaten path, well nigh two-foot broad.

Then we lighted all our matches [or gun-fuses][1] and prepared ourselves [for possible battle with Indians], concluding we were near their dwellings. But in the end, we found it to be only a path made to drive deer in (when the Indians hunt, as we supposed).

[Tombs of Mummies]

When we had marched five or six miles into the woods and could find no signs of any people, we returned again another way. And as we came into the plain ground *[returning to near Pond Village, now in North Truro, Massachusetts]*, we found a place like a grave, but it was much bigger and longer than any we had yet seen.

It was also covered with boards. So [we paused] as we mused what it should be ... and [we] resolved to dig it up. [That was] where we found first a mat, and under that, a fair bow. And there [was] another mat, and under that, a board about three quarters [of a yard] long, finely carved and painted, with three tines or broaches on the top, like a crown.

Also, between the mats, we found bowls, trays, dishes, and such like trinkets. At length, we came to a fair new mat, and under that,

---

1   Pre-lighting *matches* or fuses prepared *match-lock* guns for instant firing.

two bundles, the one bigger, the other less. We opened the greater [of the bundles] and found in it a great quantity of fine and perfect red powder—and in it, the bones and skull of a man.

The skull had fine yellow hair still on it, and some of the flesh [was] unconsumed. There was bound up with it a knife, a pack-needle, and two or three old iron things. It was bound up in a sailor's canvas cassock [or full-length topcoat] and a pair of cloth breeches. The red powder was a kind of embalmment and yielded a strong, but no[t] offensive smell. (It was as fine as any flour.)

We opened the less[er] bundle likewise and found of the same powder in it—and the bones and head of a little child. About the legs and other parts of it, was bound strings and bracelets of fine white beads. There was also by it a little bow, about three quarters [of a yard] long, and some other odd [knick]knacks.

We brought sundry of the prettiest things away with us and covered the corpses up again. After this, we digged in sundry like places, but found no more corn nor anythings else but graves.

There was variety of opinions amongst us about the embalmed person. Some thought it was an Indian Lord and King.

Others said the Indians have all black hair, and never any was seen with brown or yellow hair. Some thought it was a Christian of some special note which[1] had died amongst them, and they thus buried him to honor him. Others thought they had killed him and did it in triumph over him.

[Editor's Note: The looting of the Indian tomb contrasts with the Pilgrims' earlier respect for native graves. The *Mayflower's* crew accompanied this second exploration, possibly influencing the Pilgrims' behavior.

The Pilgrims later reported that the ship's crew, being post-medieval sailors, were often undisciplined. To keep the peace, the Pilgrims usually looked the other way; the below episode hints at the problem.]

[Indian Houses]

Whilst we were thus ranging and searching, two of the sailors, which were newly come on the shore, by chance *espied [saw]* two houses which had been lately dwelt in, but the people were gone. They [the sailors], having their [gun]-pieces and hearing nobody,

---
1 In the seventeenth century, *which* was a pronoun for both people and things.

entered the houses and took out some things—and durst [or dared] not stay, but came again [to our group of explorers] and told us. So some seven or eight of us went with them and found how we had gone within a slight shot of them before.

The houses were made with long, young sapling trees (bended and both ends stuck into the ground). They were made round, like unto an arbor, and covered down to the ground with thick and well-wrought mats.

And the door was not over a yard high, made of a mat to open. The chimney was a wide-open hole in the top, for which they had a mat to cover it close[d], when they pleased.

[The houses were tall.] One might stand and go upright in them. In the midst of them were four little *trunches*[1] [or support posts] knocked into the ground, and small sticks laid over on which they hung their pots and what they had to seeth [or boil]. Round about the fire, they lay on mats which are their beds. (The houses were double-matted. For as they were matted *without [on the outside ground]*, so were they within, with newer and fairer mats.)

In the houses, we found wooden bowls, trays and dishes, earthen pots, [and] hand-baskets made of crab shells wrought together. Also [we found] an English pail or bucket; it *wanted a bail [lacked a loop-handle]*, but it had two iron "ears" [on each side for grips].

There was also baskets of sundry sorts, bigger and some lesser, finer and some coarser. Some were curiously wrought with black and white, in pretty works.

And [we found] sundry other of their household stuff. We found also two or three deers' heads, one whereof had been newly killed, for it was still fresh. There was also a company of deers' feet stuck up in the houses; harts' horns [or deer antlers]; and eagles' claws; and sundry such, like things [that were trophies of their hunts].

There was also two or three baskets full of parched acorns, pieces of fish, and a piece of a broiled herring. We found also a little silk grass[2] and a little tobacco seed with some other seeds which we knew not. *Without [outside the houses]* was sundry bundles of flags [or iris plants] and sedge, bulrushes, and other stuff to make

---

1 Derivative of *truncheons,* a medieval word for stick or club.
2 Soft grasses used for lining rough animal skins.

mats. There was, thrust into an hollow tree, two or three pieces of venison. But we thought it fitter for the dogs than for us.

[War or Peace?]

Some of the best things, we took away with us—and left the houses standing still, as they were. [Editor's Note: This odd comment suggests that some of the explorers wanted to destroy the Indian houses, either for reasons of security, or worse, vandalism. Either way, it would have been an act of unprovoked war. William Bradford and Edward Winslow, the Pilgrim authors, may have convinced their companions, particularly the sailors, to settle for plunder, not destruction. As the below passage demonstrates, the two Pilgrims had peaceful intentions.]

So, it growing towards night, and the tide almost spent, we hasted with our things down to the shallop *[moored in the Pamet River]* and got aboard that night [on to the *Mayflower*]. [We did not plan to take the Indian goods without payment] intending to have brought some beads and other things to have left in the houses, in sign of peace and that we meant to truck [or trade] with them.

[We planned to deliver the things] but it was not done by means of our hasty coming away from Cape Cod [when we unexpectedly moved the *Mayflower* across the Bay of Cape Cod]. But, so soon as we can meet conveniently with them, we will give them full satisfaction [by repaying the Indians]. Thus, much of our second [journey of] discovery [ended on the 30th of November 1620].

[Settle Cape Cod?]

Having thus discovered this place *[Corn Hill and the Pamet River on Cape Cod in present-day Truro, Massachusetts]*, it was controversial amongst us what to do touching our abode and settling there. [See map, page 27.] Some thought it best for many reasons to abide there. [They believed] as first that there was a convenient harbor *[in the Pamet River]* for boats, though not for ships [as large as the *Mayflower*]. Secondly, good corn-ground [was nearby], ready to our hands, as we saw by experience in the goodly corn it yielded [for the Indians]. [We found a type of corn] which would again agree with the ground and be natural seed for the same.

Thirdly, Cape Cod was like[ly] to be a place of good fishing. For we saw daily great whales of the best kind for oil and bone, [which would] come close aboard our ship and, in fair weather, swim and play about us. (There was once one [special whale that visited us in the harbor]. When the sun shone warm [she] came and lay above water, as if she had been dead for a good while together—within half-a-musket-shot *[fifty yards]* of the ship.

At which, two [of our men] were prepared to shoot to see whether she would stir or no. [But] he that gave fire first—his musket flew in pieces, both stock and barrel. Yet, thanks be to God, neither he nor any man else was hurt with it, though many were thereabout. But when the whale saw her time [of leisure at end], she gave a snuff—and away!)

Fourthly, the place [on Cape Cod] was likely to be healthful, secure, and defensible. But the last and especial reason was that now the heart of winter and unseasonable weather was come upon us.

[Great storms and wind were frequent] so that we could not go upon coasting and discovery [of new places in our sailboat], without danger of losing men and boat—upon which would follow the overthrow of all—especially considering what variable winds and sudden storms do there arise.

Also, cold and wet lodging had so tainted our people, for scarce any of us were free from vehement coughs. [We feared] as if they [who were sick] should continue long in that estate, it would endanger the lives of many—and breed diseases and infection amongst us.

[Food was scarce too.] Again, we had yet some beer, butter, flesh [or meat], and other such victuals left—which would quickly be all gone. And then we should have nothing to comfort us in the great labor and toil we were like[ly] to undergo at the first [building of houses]. It was also conceived, whilst we had competent victuals, that the ship [*Mayflower*] would stay with us. But when that grew low, they would be gone and let us shift as we could.

Others again [still wanted to settle elsewhere]. [They] urged greatly the going to *Anguum* or *Angoum [Agawam or present-day Ipswich, Massachusetts]*, a place twenty leagues *[sixty miles]* off to the northwards which they had heard to be an excellent harbor for ships [and which also had] better ground and better fishing. Secondly, [they argued that] for anything we knew, there might be *hard-by us a far better seat [a much nicer place to live nearby]*, and it should be a great hindrance to seat where we should remove again.

Thirdly, the water [for drinking around Corn Hill on Cape Cod] was but in [small] ponds. And it was thought there would be none in summer, or very little. Fourthly, the water there must be fetched up a steep hill *[either Corn Hill or Old Tom's Hill]*.

[Compromise]

But to omit many reasons and replies used hereabouts, it was, in the end, concluded to make some discovery [for another place to live] within the Bay [of Cape Cod], but in no case so far as *Angoum*. Besides, Robert Coppin, our pilot [an expert on the coastal waters], made relation [or report] of a great navigable river and good harbor in the other headland of this bay [located on the western arm of land surrounding the Bay of Cape Cod].

[This other harbor was supposedly] almost right over against Cape Cod, being a right line [to the West] not much above eight leagues *[twenty-four miles]* distant, in which he had been once.[1] And because that [was where] one of the wild men—[an Indian] with whom they had some trucking [or trading for furs]—stole a harping iron [or harpoon] from them, they called it Thievish Harbor.

[Our men planned to find this harbor.] And beyond that place, they were enjoined not to go. Whereupon, a company [of our men] was chosen to go out upon a third [journey of] discovery.

[Birth and Mercy]

Whilst some were employed in this discovery, it pleased God that Mistress [Susanna] White [gave birth and] was brought a bed of a son, which was called Peregrine. **[Editor's Note: This is the first**

---

[1] Robert Coppin erred; he had never been to the place he described.

Pilgrim child born in America. His name, Peregrine, is a medieval synonym for Pilgrim—a wanderer.]

[Tuesday] the 5th day [of December 1620] – We, through God's mercy, escaped a great danger by the foolishness of a boy, one of Francis Billington's sons,[1] who, in his father's absence, had got gunpowder and had shot off a [gun]-piece or two—and made squibs [or firecrackers]. And there being *a fowling-piece charged [a loaded hunting gun]* in his father's cabin, [the boy] shot her off in the cabin.

[This started a fire], there being a little barrel of [gun]powder, half-full, scattered in and about the cabin (the fire being within four foot of the [support] bed between the decks).[2] And many flints and iron things [were] about the cabin, and many people about the fire. And yet, by God's mercy, no harm done.

[The Third Exploration]

Wednesday, the 6th of December – It was resolved [that] our discoverers should set forth, for the day before was too foul weather. And so they did, though it was well over[3] the day *ere [before]* all things could be ready. So ten of our men were appointed [to go exploring] who were of themselves willing to undertake it, to wit:
- Captain Standish, Master Carver, William Bradford, Edward Winslow, John Tilley, Edward Tilley, John Howland; and
- Three [men] of London—Richard Warren, Steven Hopkins, and Edward *Dotte [Doten]*; and
- Two of our seamen, John *Alderton [Allerton]* and Thomas English.[4]

---
1 The father was *John* Billington; the son was *Francis* Billington.
2 *Bed* could also refer to sleeping quarters, but the ship's frame is more likely.
3 The 1622 text is "it was well *ore* the day," a misprint.
4 The seamen manned the Pilgrims' *shallop* or sailboat.

Of the ship's company, there went two of the Master's Mates [or senior officers]—Master [John] Clark and Master [Robert] Coppin—the Master Gunner, and three sailors. The narration of which discovery follows, penned by one of the company [William Bradford].

[Aground]

Wednesday, the 6th of December [1620] – We set out [from the *Mayflower*], [the day] being very cold and hard weather. We were a long while [delayed by wind and tide] after we launched [in our

shallop or sailboat] from the ship, [and] before we could get clear of a sandy point *[now called Long Point, a hook-shaped peninsula]* which lay within less than a furlong *[220 yards]* of the same. In which time, two [of us] were very sick—and Edward Tilley had like to have [foundered][1] with cold. The gunner was also sick unto death, but hope of *trucking [trading with Indians]* made him to go.

And so [we] remained all that day and the next night.[2] At length, we got clear of the sandy point and got up our sails. And within an hour or two, we got under the weather [near] shore and then had smoother water and better sailing.[3] But it was very cold, for the water froze on our clothes and made them many times like coats of iron.

We sailed six or seven leagues *[eighteen to twenty-one miles]* by the shore, but saw neither river nor creek. [See map, page 62.] At length, we met with a tongue of land, being flat off from the shore, with a sandy point. We bore up to gain the point [passing it cleanly] and found there a fair *income* or *rod*—*[an inlet]* of a bay being a league *[three miles]* over at the narrowest and some two or three in length. But we made right over to the land before us and left the discovery of this *income* till the next day.

1   The 1622 text is *founded* or *sounded*, either an archaic idiom or a misprint.
2   They were delayed only one day; *next night* is either a misprint or an idiom.
3   The higher shoreline acts as a windbreak, moderating the waves.

[Wellfleet Harbor]

[Editor's Note: The explorers had sighted and temporarily passed present-day Wellfleet Harbor on Cape Cod.] As we drew near to the shore *[at Eastham, Massachusetts]*, we espied some ten or twelve Indians, very busy about a black thing. What it was, we could not tell till afterwards. They saw us and ran to and fro, as if they had been carrying something away.

[A while later] we landed a league or two *[three to six miles]* from them and had much ado to put ashore anywhere. [The water was very shallow]; it lay so full of flat sands [blocking our boat.]

When we came to shore, we made us a barricado [a wall of tree branches] and got firewood and set out our sentinels and betook us to our lodging, such as it was. We saw the smoke of the fire which the savages made that night, about four or five miles from us.

[Thursday, the 7th of December 1620] – In the morning, we divided our company [into groups]. Some eight [of our men] in the shallop, and the rest on the shore, went to discover this place *[going north a few miles to Wellfleet Harbor]*, but we found it only to be a bay without either river or creek coming into it. Yet, we deemed it to be as good an harbor as [at the tip of] Cape Cod. For they that sounded it [by measuring the depth of this new bay with knotted cord], found a ship might ride in five-fathom *[thirty-feet deep]* water.

We [who were exploring] on the land found it to be a level soil, but none of the fruitfullest. We saw two becks [or creeks] of fresh water,[1] which were the first running streams that we saw in the country (but one might stride over them).

[Strange Fish]

We found also a great fish, called a grampus *[a blackfish or pilot whale]*, dead on the sands. They in the shallop found two of them also in the bottom of the bay, dead in like sort. They [the grampus] were cast up at high water and could not get off for the frost and ice. They were some five or six paces *[fifteen to eighteen feet]* long and [had] about two inches thick of fat—and fleshed like a swine. They would have yielded a great deal of oil, if there had been time and means to have taken it.

---

1 Indian Brook (Hatches Creek) and a stream in Fresh Brook (now Wellfleet).

So, we finding nothing for our turn [of exploring the small bay], both we and our shallop returned [south along the shore of the Bay of Cape Cod]. We then directed our course along the seasands to the place where we first saw the Indians [and their black thing]. When we were there, we saw it was also a grampus which they were cutting up. They cut it into long *rands* or pieces about an *ell [forty-five inches]* long and two-handful broad. We found, here and there, a piece scattered by the way, as it seemed for haste [when the Indians ran from us].

[Our people named] this place—the most were minded [that] we should call [it] the Grampus Bay because we found so many of them there. *[The place is now called Wellfleet Harbor.]*

[Indian Houses]

We followed the track of the Indians' bare feet a good way on the sands. At length, we saw where they struck into the woods by the side of a pond *[the Great Pond in Eastham]*. As we went to view the place, one [of our men] said he thought he saw an Indian house among the trees. So [we] went up to see.

And here, we and the shallop [sailing offshore in the Bay of Cape Cod] lost sight [of] one of another till night, it being now about nine or ten o'clock [in the morning]. So we *light on [found]* a path (but saw no house) and followed a great way into the woods.

At length, we found where corn had been set, but not that year. Anon, we found a great burying place, one part whereof was encompassed with a large *palizada*[1] *[a wood fence]* like a churchyard, with young spires [or saplings] four or five yards long, set as close, one by another, as they could, two or three foot in the ground. Within it, [the enclosed yard] was full of graves, some bigger and some less. Some were also paled about [with small fences]. And others had like an Indian house made over them, but not matted.

Those graves were more sumptuous than those at Corn Hill. Yet, we digged none of them up, but only viewed them and went our way.[2] *Without [outside]* the *palizada* were graves also, but not

---

[1] Spanish word, spelled *palazado* in the 1622 text. Miles Standish may have learned the term when he fought Spanish troops in Europe in the early 1600's.
[2] The Pilgrims recognized their earlier lapse in looting Indian graves.

so costly. From this place, we went and found more corn ground, but not [planted] of this year. As we ranged, we light on four or five Indian houses which had been lately dwelt in. But they were uncovered [without roofs] and had no mats about them. Else [otherwise] they were like those we found at Corn Hill, but had not been so lately dwelt in. There was nothing left [in the houses] but two or three pieces of old mats [and] a little sedge-[grass].

Also, a little further, we found two baskets full of parched acorns hid in the ground. [We did not want them], which we supposed had been corn when we began to dig the same. We cast earth thereon again [reburying everything] and went our way.

All this while, we saw no people. We went ranging up and down till the sun began to draw low. And then we hasted out of the woods, that we might come to our shallop, which, when we were out of the woods, we espied a great way off [in the Bay of Cape Cod].

And [we] called them [the crew of the boat] to come unto us *[at the mouth of the Herring River]*, the which they did as soon as they could, for it was not yet high [tide]water. They were exceeding glad to see us. For they feared [for our safety] because they had not seen us in so long a time, thinking we would have kept by the shoreside.

So, being both weary and faint, for we had eaten nothing all that day, we fell to make our rendezvous [at the forest's edge above the beach] and get firewood, which always cost us a great deal of labor. By that time we had done, and our shallop come to us, it was within night. And we fed upon such victuals as we had and betook us to our rest—after we had set out our watch [posting armed guards].

[Alarm at Midnight]

About midnight, we heard a great and hideous cry, and our sentinel called, "Arm, Arm!" So we bestirred ourselves and shot off a couple of muskets, and [the] noise ceased. We concluded that it was a company of wolves or foxes, for one [of the sailors] told us he had heard such a noise in Newfoundland. [We went back to sleep.]

About five o'clock in the morning [on Friday, the 8th of December 1620], we began to be stirring. And two or three [of our men] which doubted whether their [gun]-pieces would go off or no, made trial of them and shot them off. But [they] thought nothing at all [of alarming those still sleeping].

After prayer, we prepared ourselves for breakfast and for a journey. And it being now the twilight in the morning, it was thought *meet [convenient]* to carry the things down to the shallop *[moored near where the Herring River empties into Cape Cod Bay]*. Some said it was not best to carry the armor down [to the boat so early]. Others said they would be readier [if they kept their weapons close]. Two or three said they would not carry theirs [to the boat] till they went themselves, but [pretended to be] mistrusting nothing at all.

As it fell out, the [tide]water not being high enough [to float the boat], they laid the things down upon the shore and came up to breakfast.

[Ambush!]

Anon, all upon a sudden, we heard a great and strange cry which we knew to be the same voices [from last night], though they varied their notes. One of our company, being abroad [in the woods], came running in and cried, "They are men! Indians, Indians!"

And withal, their arrows came flying amongst us. Our men ran out with all speed to recover their [fire]arms, as by the good Providence of God, they did.

In the meantime, Captain Miles Standish, having *a snaphance [a quick-fire gun]* ready,[1] made a shot. And after him, another [man shot also]. After they two shot, [an]other two of us were ready. But he [Captain Standish] wished us not to shoot till we could take aim. For we knew not what need we should have [of our gunpowder and bullets].

| Our first combat with the Indians. |

And there were four only of us which had their [fire]arms there ready and stood before the open side of our barricado [or wall of tree branches] which was first assaulted. They thought it best to defend it, least the enemy should take it—and our stuff—and so have the more vantage against us.

Our care was no less for the shallop [our sailboat being still at the bay shore], but we hoped all the rest [of our men] would defend it. We called unto them [at the shore] to know how it was

---

1 A mechanically-generated spark from a flint fires his gun. The other men have *match-lock* guns and need to light *matches* or fuses to fire.

with them. And they answered, "Well, well, everyone, and be of good courage!" We heard three of their [gun]-pieces go off. And the rest [of our men] called for a firebrand to light their matches [so they could fire their guns]. One [of us] took a log out of the fire, on his shoulder, and went and carried it unto them [at the shore], which was thought did not a little discourage our enemies.

[The First Encounter]

The cry of our enemies was dreadful, especially when our men ran out to recover their [fire]arms. Their note was after this manner, "*Woath woach ha ha hach woach!*[1]"

[At first, we were surprised.] Our men were no sooner come to their [fire]arms—but the enemy was ready to assault them. There was a *lusty [vigorous]* man, and no whit less valiant, who was thought to be their Captain. [This Indian] stood behind a tree within half-a-musket shot of us [fifty yards away] and there let his arrows fly at us.

He was seen to shoot three arrows, which were all avoided. For he at whom the first arrow was aimed, saw it and stooped down. And it flew over him. The rest were avoided also. [We fired back at the Indian but missed.] He stood three shots of a musket. At length, one [of us] took, as he said, full aim at him. After which, he [the Indian] gave an extraordinary cry—and away they went all!

We followed them about a quarter of a mile, but we left six [of our men behind as guards] to keep our shallop, for we were careful of our business. Then we shouted all together, two [or] several

---

1 Either arbitrary battle cries or wrongly recorded; no known translation exists.

times, and shot off a couple of muskets and so returned. This we did [so] that they might see we were not afraid of them nor discouraged. Thus, it pleased God to vanquish our enemies and give us deliverance.

By their noise, we could not guess that they were less than thirty or forty [warriors], though some thought that they were many more. Yet, in the dark of the morning, we could not so well discern them among the trees as they could see us by our fireside.

Indian Warfare, circa 1607

We took up eighteen of their arrows, which we have sent to England by Master Jones [the *Mayflower's* captain]. Some [arrows] whereof were headed with brass, others with hart's horn [deer antlers], and others with eagles' claws. Many more [kinds and numbers of arrows] no doubt were shot, for these we found were almost covered with leaves.

Yet, by the especial Providence of God, none of them either hit or hurt us, though many came close by us and on every side of us. And some coats which hung up in our barricado were shot through and through. So, after we had given God thanks for our deliverance, we took our shallop and went on our journey—and called this place, The First Encounter *[now an historic beach in Eastham]*.

[Whither Thievish Harbor?]

From hence, we intended to have sailed to the aforesaid Thievish Harbor, if we found no convenient harbor by the way. Having the wind good, we sailed all that day along the coast [of the Bay of

Cape Cod] about fifteen leagues *[forty-five miles]*, but saw neither river nor creek to put into.

After we had sailed an hour or two, it began to snow and rain, and to be bad weather. About the midst of the afternoon, the wind increased, and the seas began to be very rough. And the hinges of the rudder broke, so that we could steer no longer with it.

But two men, with much ado, were *fain [willing]* to serve [as rudders] with a couple of oars. [Nevertheless], the seas were grown so great, that we were much troubled and in great danger.

And night grew on. Anon, Master Coppin [our pilot and steersman] bade us, "Be of good cheer!"—He saw the harbor *[sighting Manomet Bluff, the southern side of Plymouth Bay]*. As we drew near, the gale being stiff, and we, bearing great sail to get in, split our mast in three pieces and were like to have cast away our shallop. Yet, by God's mercy, recovering ourselves, we had the flood [of the sea] with us and struck into the harbor.

Now he that thought that had been the place [that he discovered before] was deceived. It [was not Thievish Harbor], being a place where not any of us had been before *[Plymouth Bay]*.

And coming into the harbor, he that was our pilot [Master Coppin] did [mistakenly] bear up northward, which, if we had continued, we had been cast away [destroying our boat]. Yet, still the Lord kept us [from hitting rocks that we could scarcely see].

[The danger was great] and we bear up for an island before us *[sailing directly at a partially submerged peninsula headed by present-day Sasquish Point]*. And [our boat quickly turned away and passed by closely], recovering of that island [despite] being compassed about with many rocks, and dark night growing upon us.

[We then reached a different, safer island.] It pleased the Divine Providence that we fell upon a place of sandy ground where our shallop did ride safe and secure all that night. And coming upon a strange island, [we] kept our watch, [posting guards] all night in the rain upon that island *[now named Clark's Island, after the first man ashore, John Clark, an officer of the* Mayflower*].*

And in the morning, we marched about it and found no inhabitants at all. And here we made our rendezvous [or camp] all that day, being Saturday [the 9th of December 1620].

[Exploring Plymouth Bay]

[Sunday] 10th of December [1620] – On the Sabbath day, we rested. And on Monday [the 11th of December], we sounded the harbor [measuring its depth], and found it a very good harbor for our shipping.[1] We marched also into the land *[at present-day Plymouth, Massachusetts]* and found diverse cornfields and little running brooks—a place very good for situation [of our colony].[2]

[Tuesday, the 12th of December] – So we returned to our ship [the *Mayflower*] again [by sailing the shallop, or sailboat, directly back east across the Bay of Cape Cod], with good news to the rest of our people, which did much comfort their hearts.

---

1 The Pilgrims never found Thievish Harbor; it was not the same as Plymouth Bay, as their pilot, Robert Coppin, claimed.
2 Plymouth Rock, the legendary first stepping-stone, is not mentioned; modern Plymouth, though, recognizes December 11, Old Style, as the day of the first landing (now celebrated as Forefather's Day on December 21, New Style).

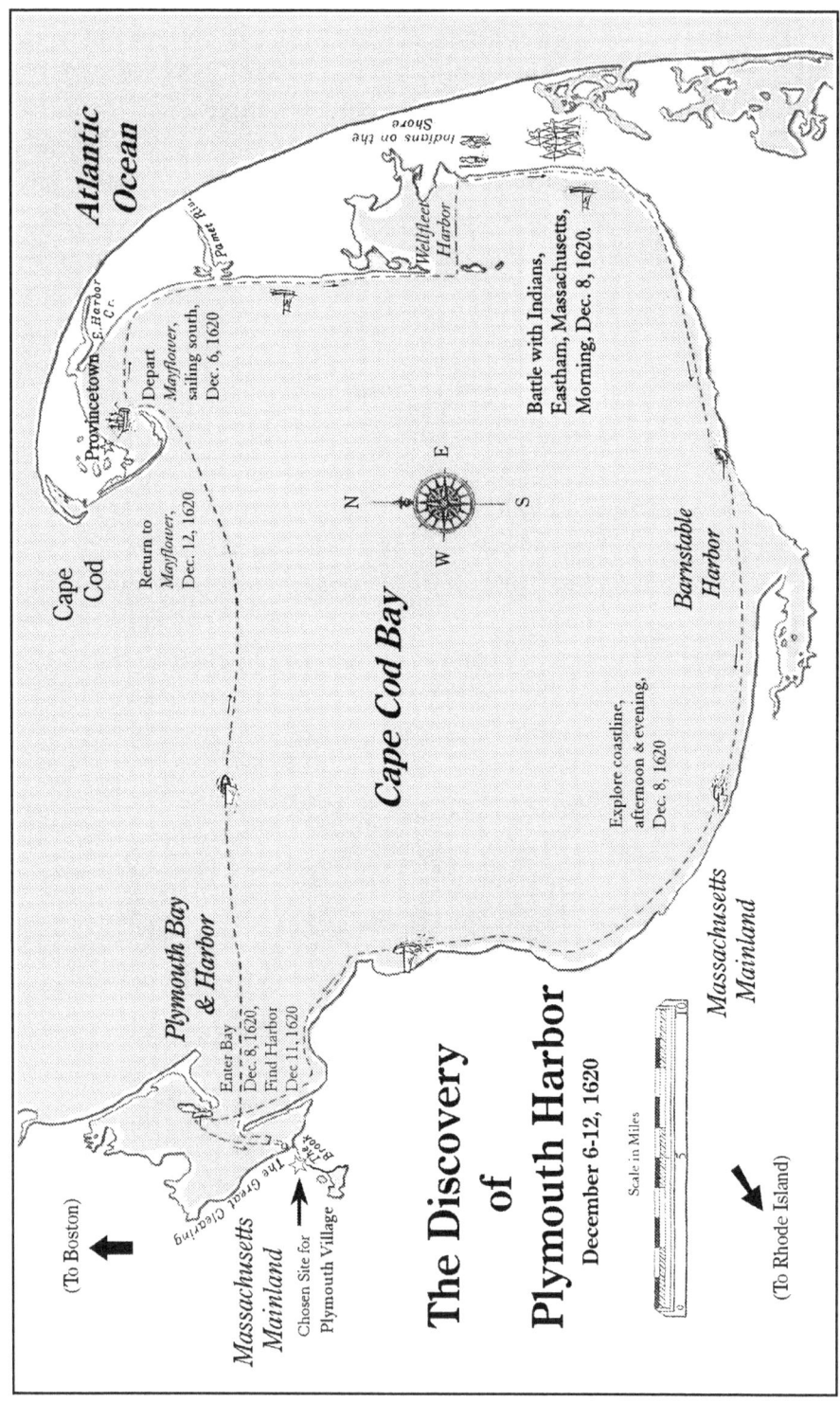

[Mayflower *Moves to Plymouth*]

On the 15th day [of December 1620], we weighed anchor [moving the *Mayflower* from Cape Cod] to go to the place we had discovered [at Plymouth Bay].[1] And coming within two leagues [six miles] of the land, we could not fetch the harbor—[we could not reach the sheltered waters] but were *fain [forced]* to put round[2] again towards Cape Cod. Our course lying west [was impossible], and the wind was at northwest [blowing to the southeast].

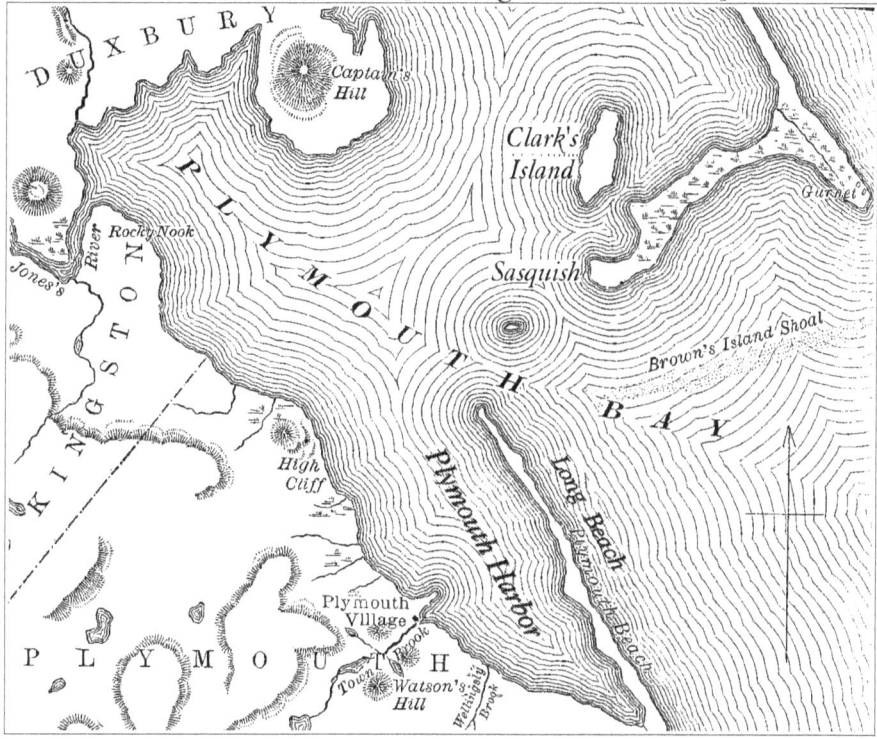

But it pleased God that the next day, being Saturday, the 16th day [of December 1620], the wind came fair. And we put to sea again and came safely into a safe harbor [at Plymouth Bay]. And within half an hour, the wind changed [but we were already secure]. So [it was] as if we had been *letted [hindered]* but a little. [If not for the early fair wind], we had gone back to Cape Cod.

This harbor [*Plymouth Bay*] is a bay greater than [at the tip of] Cape Cod, compassed with a goodly land. And in the bay [are] two

---

1 Modern annotation; the Pilgrims first mention *New Plymouth* on page 97.
2 The 1622 text is *put room,* but is likely a printer's error.

fine islands *[Clark's Island and partially submerged Sasquish peninsula]*, uninhabited, wherein are nothing but wood[s]—oaks, pines, walnut, beech, sassafras, vines, and other trees which we know not.

This bay is a most hopeful place, innumerable store of fowl, and excellent good...[?].[1] And [there] cannot but be of fish in their seasons—skate, cod, turbot, and herring. We have tasted of abundance of mussels, the greatest and best that ever we saw. Crabs and lobsters [are also], in their time, infinite. [As for the shape of this bay], it is, in fashion, like a sickle or fishhook.

[Exploration of Plymouth]

Monday, the 18th day [of December 1620][2] – We went a-land *[at present-day Plymouth, Massachusetts]*,[3] manned with the Master of the ship and three or four of the sailors. We marched along the coast in the woods, [going north] some seven or eight mile[s],[4] but saw not an Indian nor an Indian house. Only we found where formerly had been some inhabitants and where they had planted their corn. We found not any navigable river but four or five small running brooks—of very sweet fresh water—that all run into the sea.

The land—for the crust of the earth—is a spit's depth [or a shovelful deep], excellent black mold, and fat in some places. [There were also many kinds of trees]—two or three great oaks, but not very thick; pines, walnuts, beech, ash, birch, hazel, holly, asp[en], sassafras in abundance, and vines everywhere; [and] cherry trees, plum trees, and many other[s] which we know not.

Many kinds of herbs we found here in winter, [such] as strawberry leaves innumerable; sorrel, yarrow, chervil, brook-lime, liver-

---

1 Possible missing text from 1622, or a reference to the quality of the bay.
2 The 1622 text misprints the date as the *13. day*.
3 Plymouth Rock is not mentioned for December 16 or 18 (26 or 28, New Style), the last plausible dates for a first stepping-stone at Plymouth. Other Pilgrims, though, besides the distracted authors, may be the source of the legend.
4 Probable error in the 1622 text; *7 or 8 miles* is likely a misprint of *2 or 3 miles*.

wort, watercresses; great store of leeks and onions; and an excellent, strong kind of flax and hemp.

[Also] here is sand, gravel, and excellent clay (no better in the world, excellent for pots, and will wash like soap); and great store of stone, though somewhat soft; and the best water that ever we drunk (and the brooks now begin to be full of fish).

[Jones River]

That night, many [of us] being weary with marching, we went aboard again [onto the *Mayflower*]. The next morning being Tuesday, the 19th of December, we went again to discover [a new area] further *[north of present-day Plymouth]*. Some [of us] went on land, and some in the shallop *[along the coast of Plymouth Bay]*. [We went beyond] the land we found, as the former day we did, and we found a creek *[the Jones River]* and went up three English miles.[1]

[However, the creek may be] a very pleasant river at full sea-[tide]. A barque [or ocean-going ship] of thirty-ton may go up [into her mouth]. (But at low water, scarce our shallop could pass.)

[As for] this place *[present-day Kingston, Massachusetts]*, we had a great liking to plant in [and settle there]. But [we thought] that it was so far from our fishing, our principal profit, and so encompassed with woods, that we should be in much danger of *the salvages [the savages or Indians]*.[2] And our number [of people] being so little—and so much ground to clear [of trees]—we thought good to *quit and clear*[3] that place, [leaving it] till we were of more strength.

---

1 The Jones River is four to five miles north of Plymouth. The previous entry of *7 or 8 miles* without a river is inconsistent; *2 or 3 miles* was likely intended.
2 *Salvages* seems only a misspelling for *savages*, but the Pilgrims also hoped to religiously *save* the Indians. (See Appendices B & D.)
3 An idiom for abandoning land; it does not refer to clearing trees.

[Clark's Island]

Some of us, having a good mind for safety, [wanted] to plant in the greater isle *[desiring to live on Clark's Island in Plymouth Bay]*. [To explore the isle] we crossed the bay, which there *[across from the Jones River at Kingston]* is five or six miles over.

And [we] found the isle about a mile and a half [long], or two miles about [its entire shoreline]—all wooded [with many trees]. And [there was] no fresh water but two or three pits [so] that we doubted of fresh water in summer. And [the land was] so full of wood[s], as we could hardly clear so much as to serve us for corn. Besides, we judged it cold for our corn and some part very rocky. Yet, diverse [of our people] thought of it as a place defensible and of great security.

That night, we returned again a-shipboard, with resolution the next morning to settle on some of those places [as the site for our new town]. So, in the morning, after we had called on God for direction, we came to this resolution—to go presently ashore again and to take a better view of two places which we thought most fitting for us. For we could not now take time for further search or consideration—our victuals being much spent, especially our beer.[1] And it being now the 19th of December [the weather was poor].

[Founding of Plymouth Colony]

[Wednesday, 20th of December 1620] – After our landing and viewing of the places, so well as we could, we came to a conclusion, by most voices, to set on the mainland [rather than an island]. [We built] on the first place [discovered on the 11th of December], on an high ground *[in present-day Plymouth, Massachusetts, northeast of Burial Hill]* where there is a great deal of land cleared [by Indians], and hath been planted with corn three or four years ago.

And there is a very sweet brook [that] runs under the hillside—(and many delicate springs of as good water as can be drunk)—and where we may harbor our shallops and boats exceeding well. And in this brook, [there are] much good fish in their seasons; and, on the further side of the river, also much corn ground cleared. *[The brook is now called Town Brook.]*

---

1 Besides its obvious feature, beer is a rich food, high in carbohydrates.

In one field is a great hill *[present-day Burial Hill, also known as Fort Hill]*, on which we [made a] point to make a platform and plant our ordinance [of cannons], which will command all round about [and defend all directions].[1] From thence, we may see into the bay and far into the sea—and we may see thence Cape Cod.

Our greatest labor will be fetching of our [fire]wood, which is half a quarter of an English mile [away from us], but there is [only] enough so far off. [As for danger], what [native] people inhabit here, we yet know not. For as yet, we have seen none.

[The Race to Build Houses]

[Editor's Note: The Pilgrims face their most serious challenge—the weather. A bitterly cold winter is upon them. Their cramped, unheated ship, the *Mayflower*, cannot provide adequate shelter. However, building houses further exposes the Pilgrims to the dangerous cold. Nevertheless, warm houses are the only way to avoid a wintry death. A desperate race with time commences.]

So there *[at present-day Plymouth]*, we made our rendezvous and a place [to camp that night] for some of our people (about twenty), resolving in the morning to come all ashore and to build houses. But the next morning being Thursday, the 21st of December [1620], it was [so] stormy and wet that we could not go ashore.

---

1   The 165-foot Burial Hill is the highest of Plymouth and a natural fortification.

And those that remained there all night could do nothing, but were wet, not having daylight enough to make them a sufficient court-of-guard [or guardhouse] to keep them dry.

All that night, it blew and rained extremely. It was so tempestuous that the shallop could not go [from the *Mayflower*] on land so soon as was *meet [necessary]*, for they had no victuals on land.

About eleven o'clock [that night], the shallop went off, with much ado, with provision [for our people on shore] but could not return [because of the wind]. It blew so strong and was such foul weather, that we were forced to let fall our anchor[s] and ride with three anchors ahead.[1]

Going Ashore

Friday, the 22nd [of December 1620] – The storm still continued [such] that we could not get a-land, nor they [who were ashore] come to us aboard [the *Mayflower*]. This morning, goodwife *[Mary] Allerton*[2] was delivered of a son, but dead-born.

Saturday, the 23rd [of December] – So many of us as could, went on shore, felled and carried timber [cutting down trees and hauling logs] to provide themselves stuff for building.

---

1 The 1622 text is "three anchors *an head*," either a misspelling or quaint speech.
2 *Goodwife* is a quaint title for a married woman. Mary and Issac *Allerton* were a prominent Pilgrim couple; the 1622 text prints their name as *Alderton*.

Sunday, the 24th [of December 1620] – Our people on shore heard a cry of some savages (as they thought), which caused an alarm. And [they rushed] to stand on their guard, expecting an assault, but all was quiet.

[First Christmas]

Monday, the 25th day [of December 1620] – We went on shore —some [of us] to fell timber, some to saw, some to rive [crafting mortise-and-tenon joints of house frames], and some to carry [the lumber]. So no man rested all that day.

But towards night, some as they [who] were at work, heard a noise of some Indians, which caused us all to go to our muskets. But we heard no further. So we came aboard again [to the *Mayflower*] and left some twenty [of our men ashore] to keep the court-of-guard. That night we had a sore storm of wind and rain.

Monday, the 25th [of December, evening] – [The day] being Christmas Day, we began to drink water [mixed with liquor] aboard [the *Mayflower*]. But at night, the Master [Christopher Jones, the ship's captain] caused us to have some beer. And so, on board, we had diverse times—now and then, some beer—but on shore [they had] none at all.

Tuesday, the 26th [of December 1620] – It was foul weather [such] that we could not go ashore.

Wednesday, the 27th [of December] – We went to work again.

Thursday, the 28th of December – So many as could, went to work on the hill where we purposed to build our platform for our ordinance [of cannons], and which doth command all the plain [of land] and the bay. And from whence, we may see far into the sea.

[The Town Street]

And [our town] might be easier impaled [or encircled with a wall of timbers] having [only] two rows of houses and a fair street. So, in the afternoon, we went to measure out the grounds *[on a modest bluff called Cole's Hill, below the harborside of Burial Hill].*

And first, we took notice how many families they [our people] were, willing [or requesting] all single men that had no wives to

join with some family as they thought fit. That [was] so we might build fewer houses, which was done.

And we reduced them to nineteen families. To greater families [with more people], we allotted larger plots [of land]; to every person [we set aside] ground that was] half a pole in breadth *[eight and one-quarter feet wide]* and three in length *[forty-nine and one-half feet long].*

And so [random] lots were cast[1] where every man should lie [in our new town], which was done and staked out. We thought this proportion [of land] was large enough, at the first, for houses and gardens—[and] to impale them round [with a wall]—considering the weakness of our people, many of them growing ill with colds.

For our former [journeys of] discoveries in frost and storms—and the wading [in cold water] at Cape Cod—had brought much weakness amongst us, which increased so everyday, more and more, and after[wards] was the cause of many of their deaths.

---

1 *"Lots* were cast," could also mean creating parcels of land, i.e., property *lots.* However, a random lottery for the best locations is a better interpretation.

Street Map
Plymouth Colony, 1621

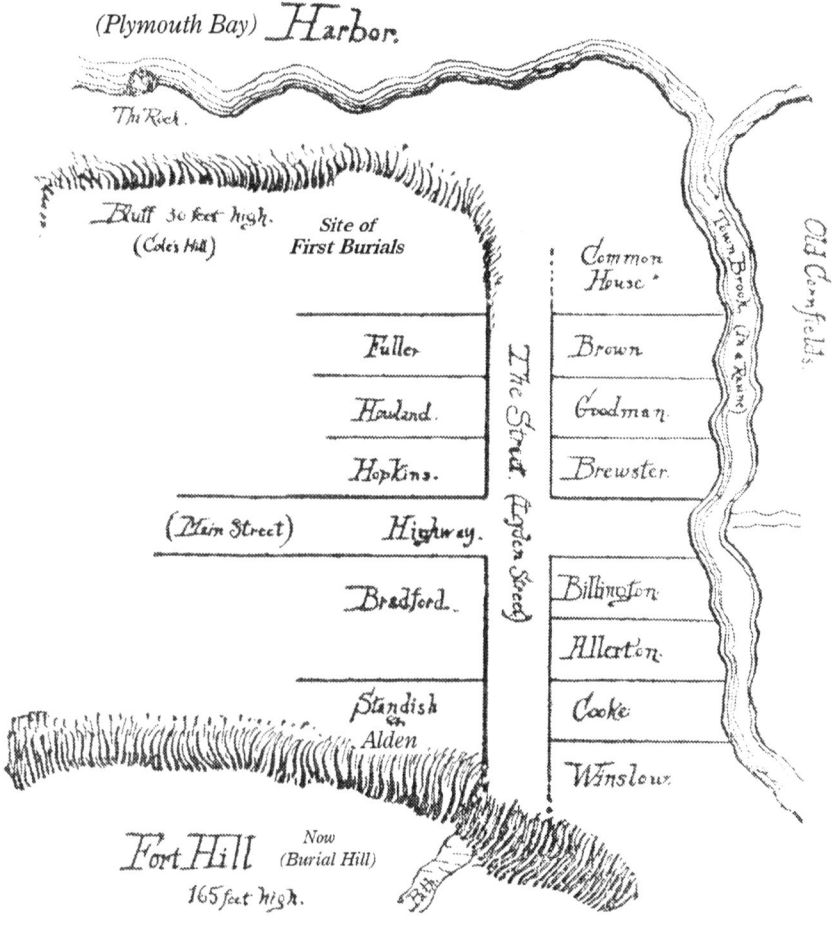

In 1920, the Tricentennial of the Pilgrims' arrival in America, the author John Goodwin drew this map of Plymouth Village with likely locations of various families.

[Cold & Wet]

Friday and Saturday [29th and 30th of December 1620] – We fitted ourselves for our labor. But our people on shore were much troubled and discouraged with rain and wet (that day being very stormy and cold).

We saw great smokes of fire made by the Indians about six or seven miles from us *[to the South toward present-day Telegraph Hill]*, as we conjectured.

Monday, the first of January [1621] – We went *betimes [early]* to work. We were much hindered because [the *Mayflower*], in lying so far off from the land, and *fain [being compelled]* to go as the tide served, [often changed position so] that we lost much time.[1]

For our ship *drew so much water*—*[the* Mayflower's *180-ton hull protruded far below the waterline]*—that she lay [far from land in deep water] a mile and almost a half off. (Though a ship of seventy or eighty ton at high [tide]water may come to the shore.)

[Fires of the Indians]

Wednesday, the 3rd of January – Some of our people [were] being abroad [in the forest] to get and gather *thatch [wild straw from grasses and reeds]*. [In the distance] they saw great fires of the Indians and were at their cornfields. Yet [we] saw none of the savages nor had seen any of them since we came to this bay *[at Plymouth]*.

---

1 At low tide, the *Mayflower* moved further offshore to avoid grounding. This slowed offloading of supplies, which were ferried to shore by small boats.

Thursday, the 4th of January [1621] – Captain Miles Standish, with four or five more [of our men], went to see if they could meet with any of the savages in that place where the fires were made. They went to some of their houses (but not lately inhabited); yet could they not meet with any [Indians].

As they came home, they shot at an eagle and killed her, which was excellent meat. It was hardly to be discerned from mutton.

[Fishing]

Friday, the 5th of January – One of the sailors found alive upon the shore an herring, which the Master [the ship's captain] had to his supper [and] which put us in hope of fish. But as yet, we had got but one cod—we wanted small hooks [to catch fish properly].

Saturday, the 6th of January – Master [Christopher] Martin was very sick and, to our judgment, [had] no hope of life. So Master Carver [our leader] was sent for, to come aboard [the *Mayflower*] to speak with him about his *accompts [accounts]*.[1] [Master Carver], who came the next morning [met with Master Martin on Sunday, the 7th of January 1621, before his death the next day].

---

1 *Accompts* refers to financial accounts; Christopher Martin was "governor" or administrator of the *Mayflower*. He also led a group of non-Pilgrims, so-called "strangers" who came to America to improve their living standards. The Pilgrims came primarily for religious reasons, i.e., to build a better world.

Monday, the 8th day of January [of 1621], was a very fair day, and we went betimes to work.

Master Jones [the *Mayflower's* captain] sent the shallop [to sea, equipping the sailboat's crew with fishing lines] as he had formerly done to see where fish could be got. They had a great storm at sea and were in some danger. At night, they returned with three great seals and an excellent good cod, which did assure us that we should have plenty of fish shortly.

This day, Francis Billington, having the week before seen (from the top of a tree on an high hill) a great [inland] sea, as he thought, went with one of the Master's Mates [a senior officer of the *Mayflower*] to see it. They went three miles and then came to a great water, divided into two great lakes, the bigger of them five or six miles in circuit, and in it, an isle of a cable-length *[608-feet]* square. The other [lake is] three miles in compass. In their estimation, they are fine freshwater—full of fish and fowl.

[The lakes form the present-day Billington Sea]; a brook issues from it *[now called Town Brook and which flows all the way to Plymouth].* It *[the Sea]* will be an excellent help for us in time.

They [our people] found seven or eight Indian houses [near the lakes], but not lately inhabited. When they saw the houses, they were in some fear, for they were but two persons and one [gun]-piece.

[Common House]

Tuesday, the 9th [of] January, was a reasonable fair day. And we went to labor that day in the building of our town—in two rows of houses for more safety. We divided by lot the plot of ground whereon to build our town.[1] After the proportion [was] formerly allotted, we agreed that every man should build his own house, thinking, by that course, men would make more haste than working in common.

The common house[2]—in which for the first [weeks], we made our rendezvous—being near finished, [needed or] wanted only covering [for the roof], it being about twenty-foot square. [We directed] some should make mortar, and some gather thatch [from

---

1 This reiterates an entry of December 28, 1620.
2 The common house later sheltered the sick, food, and gunpowder.

wild straw of grass and reeds], so that in four days, half of it was thatched [with a roof of bundled straw].

Frost and foul weather hindered us much this time of the year. Seldom could we work half the week.

Thursday, the 11th [of January 1621] – William Bradford, being at work (for it was a fair day), was vehemently taken with a grief and pain, and *so shot to his huckle-bone—[so crippled with agony in his hip-bone]*[1]—it was doubted [of his survival].

[We feared] that he would have instantly died. He got cold in the former discoveries, especially the last [exploration to find our new home], and felt some pain in his ankles *by times [now and then]*. But he grew a little better towards night and, in time, through God's mercy in the use of [medical] means, recovered.

[Disappeared]

Friday the 12th [of January] – We went to work, but about noon, it began to rain [so hard] that it forced us to give over work [halting construction of our houses].

[Also] this day, two of our people put us in great sorrow and care. [The trouble began when] there was *[sic]* four [of our men] sent to gather and cut thatch in the morning. And two of them, John Goodman and Peter Browne, having cut thatch all the forenoon, went to a further place and willed [or requested] the other two to bind up that which was cut and to follow them [a little later].

So they did [walk away into the forest], being about a mile and a half from our plantation. But when the two [other men] came after [to look for Goodman and Browne], they could not find them nor hear anything of them at all—though they [hollered or halloed][2] and shouted as loud as they could.

So they returned to the company [of our people] and told them of it. Whereupon Master Carver[3] [our leader] and three or four more [of our men] went to seek them, but could hear nothing of them. So they, [after] returning, sent more [men to search], but that night they could hear nothing at all of them. The next day,

---

1 Possibly rheumatism, or rheumatoid arthritis, induced by stress and cold.
2 Replaces the malapropism *hallowed,* i.e., *to make holy,* in the 1622 text.
3 The 1622 text is *Master Leaver,* a misprint.

they armed ten or twelve men out [as a military force], verily thinking the Indians had surprised them [our lost men].

They went seeking seven or eight miles, but could neither see nor hear anything at all. So they returned [without finding our men], with much discomfort to us all.

[Lost & Found]

[We learned later that] these two that were missed [got lost]. At dinner time, [they often] took their meat in their hands and would go walk and refresh themselves. So, going a little off [that first day], they find a lake of water *[near the present-day Billington Sea].*

And having a great *mastiff* ...[1] *[a female hunting dog]* with them, and a [cocker] spaniel, [the men got into a hunt]. By the waterside, they found a great deer. The dogs chased him, and they [our two men] followed so far as they lost themselves and could not find the way back.

Mastiff Dog, circa 1650

They wandered all that afternoon, being wet. And at night, it did freeze and snow. They were slenderly appareled, and had no weapons but each one his sickle [the curved steel blade that they used to harvest straw]. Nor [had they] any victuals.

[They then sought houses of the Indians.] They ranged up and down, and [yet] could find none of the *salvages'* habitations.

When it drew to night, they were much perplexed. For they could find neither harbor nor meat, but in frost and snow were forced to make the earth their bed and *the element[s] their covering* —*[they were completely exposed to the weather]*.

And another thing did very much terrify them. They heard, as they thought, two lions roaring exceedingly for a long time together. And [there was] a third [lion] that they thought was very near

---

1 Mastiffs are traditional English dogs, dating back thousands of years. The Pilgrims also mentioned a medieval vernacular for the dog; the term now has a secondary, vulgar implication, not intended by the Pilgrims. To avoid confusion, this annotated edition substitutes a neutral definition.

them. So, not knowing what to do, they resolved to climb up into a tree as their safest refuge, though that would prove an intolerable, cold lodging. So they stood at the tree's root, [hoping] that when the lions came, they might take their opportunity of climbing up. The ... *[mastiff hunting dog]¹* they were *fain [required]* to hold by the neck—for she would have been gone to the lion [to fight him].

North American Panther

But it pleased God, so to dispose that the wild beasts came not. So they walked up and down under the tree all night. It was an extreme cold night.

So soon as it was light, they travailed again [hiking arduously across the land], passing by many lakes and brooks and woods. And, in one place, [they found] where the *salvages* had burnt [the forest] the space of five miles in length, which is a fine champion country, and even [or relatively flat]. *[They were near the Great South Pond, four or five miles south of Plymouth.]*

In the afternoon, it pleased God [that] from an high hill, they discovered the two isles in the bay [as landmarks pointing homeward]. And so that night, [they] got to the plantation, being ready to faint with travail and want of victuals—and almost famished with cold.

John Goodman was *fain [required]* to have his shoes cut off his feet; they were so swelled with cold. And it was a long while after, *ere [before]* he was able to go [exploring again].

[The House Fire]

Those on the shore were much comforted at their return. But they on shipboard [being unaware] were grieved as deeming them lost. But the next day, being the 14th of January [1621]—in the morning about six of the clock, the wind being very great—they on shipboard spied their great, new rendezvous on fire [the common house being ablaze ashore], which was to them a new discomfort.

[They were] fearing, because of the supposed loss of the men, that the *salvages* had fired them [our houses]. Neither could they

---
1 See previous footnote.

[on ship] presently go to them [on shore] for want of [tide]water [to float boats]. But after three-quarters of an hour, they went, as they had purposed the day before to keep the Sabbath on shore. Because now, there [on land] was the greater number of people [rather than on the ship].

At their landing, they heard good tidings of the return of the two men, and that the house was fired occasionally by a spark that flew into the thatch [or straw covering the roof], which instantly burnt it all up. But the [wood frame of the] roof stood, and little hurt.

The most [near] loss was Master Carver's and William Bradford's [respectively governor and deputy governor], who then lay sick in bed. And if they had not risen with good speed, [they] had been blown up with [gun]powder.

But through God's mercy, they had no harm. The house was as full of beds [of the sick] as they could lie *[sic]* one by another, and their muskets charged [with gunpowder and bullets]. But blessed be God, there was no harm done.

Monday, the 15th day [of January 1621] – It rained much all day [so] that they on shipboard could not go on shore; nor they on shore do any labor but were all wet.

Tuesday, Wednesday, Thursday [16th through 18th of January] were very fair, sunshiny days, as if it had been in April. And our people, so many as were in health, wrought cheerfully.

The 19th day [of January] – We resolved to make a shed to put our common provision in, of which some were already set on shore. But at noon, it rained [so] that we could not work.

[Dog versus Wolves]

This day, in the evening, John Goodman went abroad [into the forest] to use his lame feet that were pitifully ill with the cold he had got. Having a little spaniel with him [he had to fight off wild animals]. A little way from the plantation, two great wolves ran af-

ter the dog. The dog ran to him [John Goodman] and betwixt his legs for succor. He had nothing in his hand, but took up a stick and threw at one of them and hit him. And they [the wolves] presently ran both away but came again. He [John Goodman] got *a paleboard [a long garden stake]* in his hand [to use as a spear]. And they [the wolves] sat both on their tails, grinning at him a good while—and [only later] went their way and left him.

[Winter's Depth]

Saturday, 20th [of January 1621] – We made up our shed for our common goods.

Sunday, the 21st – We kept our [Sabbath] meeting on land.[1]

Monday, the 22nd – Was a fair day. We wrought on our houses and in the afternoon carried up our hogsheads of meal [or barrels of flour] to our common storehouse. The rest of the week, we followed our business likewise.

Monday, the 29th – In the morning, [it was] cold frost and sleet, but after[wards], reasonably fair. Both the longboat and the shallop brought our common goods on shore.

Tuesday and Wednesday, 30th and 31st of January – [It was] cold, frosty weather and sleet, [so] that we could not work. In the morning, the Master [the *Mayflower's* captain] and others saw two savages that had been on the island near our ship *[the "island" being present-day Long Beach, now a peninsula]*.

What they came for, we could not tell. They were going so far back again [into the forest] before they were descried—[our people noticed them far too late]—that we could not speak with them.

Sunday, the 4th of February [1621], was very wet and rainy, with the greatest gusts of wind that ever we had since we came forth. That [disturbed us], though we rid *[sic]* in a very good harbor. Yet

---

1 William Brewster, a church Elder, usually conducted religious services. The Pilgrims, though, discreetly never mention his name; the English King sought Mr. Brewster's arrest for advocating religious reform.

we were in danger because our ship was light, the goods taken out, and she unballasted [without weights to balance her upright].¹ [The storm was very violent] and it caused much *daubing [the clay sealing the wood siding]* of our houses to fall down.

Friday, the 9th [of February] – Still, the cold weather continued [such] that we could do little work. That afternoon, our little house for our sick people was [again] set on fire by a spark that kindled in the roof, but no great harm was done.

That evening, the Master [the *Mayflower's* captain], going ashore, killed five geese, which he friendly² distributed among the sick people. He found also a good deer killed [by Indians]. The savages had cut off the horns, and a wolf was eating of him. How he [the deer] came there, we could not conceive.

[**Editor's Note:** It was rare for Indians to kill animals only for souvenirs, e.g., "horns" or antlers. Instead, local natives may have deposited the deer where the half-starved settlers would find it. Indians were secretly observing the Pilgrims at the time and may have taken pity upon the sickly, suffering newcomers.]

[Indians Approach]

Friday, the 16th day [of February] was a fair day, but the northerly wind continued, which continued the frost. This day [in the] afternoon, one of our people being *a-fowling [bird hunting]* and having taken a stand by a creekside in the reeds about a mile and an

---

1   Empty ships float high on the water and are vulnerable to capsizing.
2   Quaint use of *friendly* as an adverb, similar to "he *kindly* distributed..."

half from our plantation, there came by him twelve Indians marching towards our plantation.

And in the woods, he heard the noise of many more [Indians]. He lay close [to the ground] till they were passed. And then, with what speed he could, he went home and gave the alarm.

So the people abroad in the woods returned and armed themselves, but saw none of them [the Indians having disappeared into the forest]. Only toward the evening, they [the Indians] made a great fire about the place where they were first discovered.

Captain Miles Standish and Francis Cook, being at work in the woods [and quickly] coming home, left their tools behind them. But before they returned [to the forest to retrieve them], their tools were taken away by the savages.

This coming of the savages gave us occasion to keep more strict watch and to make *our pieces and furniture ready—[we prepared our guns and munitions]*—which, by the moisture and rain, were out of temper.

Saturday, the 17th day [of February] – In the morning, we called a meeting for the establishing of military orders amongst ourselves. And we chose Miles Standish our captain and gave him authority of command in affairs.

And, as we were in consultation hereabouts, two savages presented themselves upon the top of an hill *[Watson's Hill or Strawberry Hill]* over against our plantation [directly in front of us], about a quarter of a mile and less. [See map, page 63.] And they made signs unto us, to come unto them. We likewise made signs unto them, to come to us. Whereupon we armed ourselves and stood ready.

And [we] sent two [of our men] over the brook towards them, to wit, Captain Standish and Steven Hopkins, who went towards them. [Of our two men] only one of them had a musket, which they laid down on the ground in their sight, in sign of peace and to parley with them. But the savages would not tarry their coming [and ran away as our men approached].

A noise of a great many more [of the Indians] was heard behind the hill, but no more came in sight. This caused us to plant our great ordinances [of cannons] in places most convenient.

Wednesday, the 21st of February [1621] – The Master [the *Mayflower's* captain] came on shore with many of his sailors and brought with him one of the great [cannon]-pieces, called a *minion*. And [they] helped us to draw it up the hill *[present-day Burial Hill]* with another piece that lay on shore. And [we] mounted them and *a saker*[1] *[a large siege cannon]* and *two bases [two small cannons]*.

He [the *Mayflower's* captain] brought with him a very fat goose to eat with us. And we [also] had a fat crane and a mallard and a dried *neats-tongue [cow-tongue]*. And so we were kindly and friendly together.

[Editor's Note: The Pilgrims were well-armed for a religious settlement. Their cannons weighed up to a thousand pounds each, firing cast-iron balls up to four inches in diameter. The artillery was necessitated by the annihilation of several European settlements in America, including the "Lost Colony" at Roanoke Island in 1590; the Pilgrims were determined not to suffer the same fate.

The mounting of cannons on February 21, 1621, also marked the tragic peak of a deadly winter epidemic. At least four people died that day of an influenza-like disease, including William White, father of the first baby born to the Pilgrims; and William Mullins, father of Priscilla Mullins, the young woman immortalized by the poet Henry Longfellow in his legendary epic, *The Courtship of Miles Standish* (since restored as *The Romance of Pilgrims*).

The epidemic would not run its full course for several more weeks, claiming 50 lives, half of the original 102 settlers. Women were particular-

---

1   The 1622 text misprints *saker* as *saller*.

ly vulnerable. The dead eventually included Rose Standish, wife of Captain Miles Standish, military advisor; Elizabeth Winslow, wife of Edward Winslow, an author of this report; and Ann Tilley, wife of Edward Tilley, one of the first explorers of Cape Cod. (Mr. Tilley also perished.)

In addition, on February 25, 1621, Mary Allerton died. She was the wife of Issac Allerton, whose baby was still-born two months earlier. The forlorn mother shared her infant's fate only days before a life-giving warmth arrived.]

Walking to Religious Services

[An Early Spring]

Saturday, the 3rd of March [1621] – The wind was [from the] South, the morning misty, but towards noon, warm and fair weather. The birds sang in the woods most pleasantly. At one of the clock, it thundered, which was the first we heard in that country. It was strong and great claps, but short. But after an hour, it rained very sadly till midnight.

Wednesday, the 7th of March – The wind was full [from the] East, [the weather being] cold but fair. That day, Master Carver [our governor], with five other[s], went to the great ponds *[present-day Billington Sea or Great South Pond, several miles to the southwest]*, which seem to be excellent fishing places. All the way they went, [on the ground] they found it exceedingly beaten and haunted with [tracks of] deer—but they saw none [of the animals].

Amongst other fowl, they saw one [that was] a milk-white fowl, with a very black head. [Back in our fields] this day, some garden seeds were sown.

[A Friend]

Friday, the 16th [of March 1621] – A fair, warm day towards [or good weather for now]. This morning, we determined to conclude of the military orders which we had began to consider of before, but were interrupted by the savages, as we mentioned formerly.

And whilst we were busied hereabout, we were interrupted again. For there presented himself a savage, which caused an alarm. He very boldly came all alone and along the houses, straight to the rendezvous [our fortified camp at the common house], where we intercepted him, not suffering him to go in, as undoubtedly he would out of his boldness.

[The Indian's name was *Samoset*.] He saluted us in English and bade us welcome. For he had learned some broken English amongst the Englishmen that came to fish at *Monchiggon [present-day Monhegan Island off the coast of Maine]*. And [he] knew by name, the most of the Captains, Commanders, and Masters [of the fishing ships] that usually come [to New England].

He was a man free in speech—so far as he could express his mind—and of a *seemly [handsome]* carriage. We questioned him of many things; he was the first savage we could meet withal. He said he was not of these parts but of Moratiggon *[another spelling of Monhegan Island]* and [was] one of the *sagamores* or lords thereof (and had been eight months in these parts).

[His homeland was not far away]—it lying hence a day's sail with a great wind, and five days by land. He discoursed of the whole country and of every province, and of their *sagamores* and their number of men and strength.

The wind beginning to rise a little, we cast a horseman's coat about him, for he was stark naked—only a leather [belt] about his waist, with a fringe about a span long *[nine inches]* or little more.

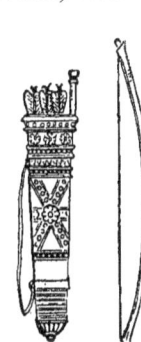

(He had a bow and two arrows, the one headed [with a sharp point] and the other unheaded.)

He was a tall, straight man. The hair of his head [was] black—long behind, only short before [on his forehead]—[but] none on his face at all.

He asked [for] some beer, but we gave him *strong water [alcoholic liquor]*—and biscuit and butter and cheese and pudding and a piece of a mallard—all which he liked well and had been acquainted with such amongst the English

He told us the place where we now live is called *Patuxet,* and that about four years ago, all the inhabitants died of an extraordinary plague—and there is neither man, woman, nor child remaining, as indeed we have found none. So, as there is none to hinder our possession or to lay claim unto it [the land is ours].

All the afternoon, we spent in communication with him. We would gladly have been rid of him at night [for our safety], but he was not willing to go this night.

Then we thought to carry him on shipboard, wherewith he was well content and went into the shallop [to be ferried over to the *Mayflower*]. But the wind was high and [tide]water scant [so] that it could not return back [the same night]. [Rather], we lodged him that night at Steven Hopkin's house and watched him. The next day, he went away back to the *Massasoits¹* *[the Wampanoag or Pokanoket Indians]* from whence he said he came, [and] who are our next, bordering neighbors. They are sixty strong, as he sayeth.

[The Nausite *Indians]*

The *Nausites* [an Indian tribe on Cape Cod] are as near southeast of them *[the Pokanoket Indians]* and are a hundred strong. And those *[Nausites]* were they of whom our people were encountered [in combat], as we before related. They are much incensed and provoked against the English.

And about eight months ago, [the *Nausites*] slew three Englishmen—and two more hardly escaped by flight to *Monhiggon* *[Monhegan Island]*. They were [sent from England by] Sir Ferdinando Gorge[s]²—his men *[Captain Thomas Dermer and crew]*—as this savage told us, as he did likewise [tell] of the *huggerie*, that is, fight that our discoverers had with the *Nausites* [in December 1620].

And [we spoke] of our tools that were taken out of the woods, which we willed him [or firmly asked] should be brought again. Otherwise, we would right ourselves [by seeking compensation].

These people are ill-affected towards the English by reason of one [Thomas] Hunt, a Master of a ship, who deceived the people and got them [as captives] *under color of trucking with them [while pretending to trade for furs]*. [He took] twenty out of this very place where we inhabit—and seven men from the *Nausites*—and carried them away and sold them for slaves like a wretched man (for twenty pound a man) that cares not what mischief he doth for his profit.

Saturday [the 17th of March] – In the morning, we dismissed the *salvage* [who was named *Samoset*] and gave him a knife, a bracelet, and a ring. He promised, within a night or two, to come again and to bring with him some of the *Massasoits*, our [Indian] neighbors, with such beavers' skins as they had to truck [or trade] with us.

---

1   The tribe's name was *Wampanoag* or *Pokanoket;* its leader was *Massosoit*.
2   In 1620, the English King granted Sir Fernando Gorges the exclusive right to colonize Massachusetts. Fortuitously, the Pilgrims' agent in London, Robert Cushman, secured from Sir Gorges a land grant in their name.

[More Indians]

Saturday and Sunday [17th and 18th of March 1621] were reasonable fair days. On this [Sun]day, came again the savage *[Samoset]* —and brought with him five other, tall proper men. They had every man a deer's skin on him. And the principal of them [or their leader] had a wildcat's skin, or such like, on the one arm.

They had, most of them, long *hosen [leather leggings]* up to their groins, close-made; and above their groins to their waist [was] another [piece of] leather. (They were altogether like the Irish trousers.)

They are of complexion like our English gypsies. No hair or very little [was] on their faces; on their heads, long hair to their shoulders, only cut before [as short hair in front]. Some [had raised hair on their foreheads], trussed-up before with a feather, broad-wise like a fan. Another [had] a fox-tail hanging out [the back of his head].

These [Indians] left [their weapons outside of our camp], according to our charge given him *[Samoset]* before. Their bows and arrows [were] a quarter of a mile from our town.

We gave them *entertainment [hospitality]*, as we thought was fitting them. They did eat liberally of our English victuals. They made semblance unto us of friendship and amity. They song *[sic]* and danced, after their manner [and] like antics.

They brought with them—in a thing like a bowcase which the principal [or leader] of them had about his waist—a little of their corn pounded to powder, which, put to a little water, they eat. He [also] had a little tobacco in a bag, but none of them *drunk*[1], but when he *listed—[none smoked tobacco, unless their leader did so]*.

Some of them had their faces painted black from the forehead to the chin, four or five fingers broad. Others [painted their faces] after other fashions, as they liked.

---

1 An odd idiom of the era; to *drink* tobacco, was to smoke it.

They brought three or four skins [or furs of animals], but we would not truck [or trade] with them at all that day but wished them to bring more—and we would truck for all—which they promised within a night or two. And [they gladly] would leave these behind them, though we were not willing they should.

And they brought us all our tools again, which were taken in the woods in our men's absence.

So, because of the day [being Sunday, the Sabbath for our religious services], we dismissed them so soon as we could. But *Samoset*, our first acquaintance, either was sick or feigned himself so, and would not go with them. And [he] stayed with us till Wednesday morning [the 21st of March].

Then we sent him to them. [We wanted] to know the reason [why] they came not [to visit again] according to their words. And we gave him an hat; a pair of stockings and shoes; a shirt and a piece of cloth to tie about his waist.

[Gifts for the Indians]

The Sabbath day [Sunday, 18th of March 1621] when we sent them from us, we gave every one of them some trifles, especially the principal of them [their leader]. We carried them [our gifts], along with our [fire]arms, to the place where they left their bows and arrows, whereat they were amazed. And two of them [being afraid of our guns] began to slink away, but that [stopped when] the other [Indian] called them. When they took their arrows, we bade them farewell, and they were glad. And so with many thanks given us, they departed—with promise they would come again.

Monday and Tuesday [19th and 20th of March 1621] proved fair days. We digged our grounds and sowed our garden seeds.

Wednesday [the 21st of March] – A fine, warm day. We sent away *Samoset*.

[Third Visit by Indians]

That day [21st of March], we had again a meeting to conclude of laws and orders for ourselves; and to confirm those military orders that were formerly propounded and twice broken off by the savages coming. But so we were again [visited]—the third time. For after we had been an hour together, on the top of the hill over against us [or directly in front of our settlement], two or three savages presented themselves that made semblance of daring us, as we thought.

So Captain Standish, with another [of our men] with their muskets, went over to them. [They went] with two of the Master's Mates [two senior officers of the *Mayflower*] that follows them without [fire]arms, having two muskets with them [for all four men].

[As for the Indians], they whetted and rubbed their arrows and strings, and made show of defiance. But when our men drew near them, they ran away. Thus, we were again interrupted by them.

[For our better defense, we hurried to get more people on shore from the *Mayflower*.] This day, with much ado, we got our carpenter—that had been long sick of the scurvy—to fit our shallop to fetch all from aboard.

[Squanto]

Thursday, the 22nd of March [1621], was a very fair, warm day. About noon, we met again about our public business. But we had scarce been an hour together, but *Samoset* came again—and [with another Indian] *Squanto*.

[*Squanto* was] the only native of *Patuxat [or Patuxet]* where we now inhabit, [and] who was one of the twenty captives that by Hunt [the English sea captain] were carried away [into foreign slavery]. And [*Squanto*] had been in England and dwelt in Cornhill [an area of London][1] with Master John Slany, a merchant. (And [*Squanto*] could speak a little English.)

[*Samoset* and *Squanto* came with] with three others, and they brought with them some few skins [of animals] to truck; and some red herrings, newly taken and dried, but not salted.

And [they] signified unto us that their great *sagamore*, *Massasoit,* was hard-by— [the Indians' king was nearby]—with *Quadequina*, his brother, and all their men. They could not well express in English what they would [want]. But after an hour, the king came to the top of an hill over against us—and had in his train [behind him] sixty men [so] that we could well behold them, and they, us.

[First Meeting]

We were not willing to send our governor [John Carver] to them; and they, unwilling to come to us. So *Squanto* went again unto him [the Indian's leader].

[*Massasoit*, the Indian king, spoke to *Squanto*] who brought word that we should send one to parley with him, which we did, which was Edward Winslow. [We wanted] to know his mind [that of the Indian king] and to signify the mind and will of our governor, which was to have trading and peace with him.

We sent to the king a pair of knives and a copper chain with a jewel attached.[2] To *Quadequina* [his brother], we sent likewise a knife and a jewel to hang in his ear; and withal, a pot of *strong water [alcoholic liquor]*, a good quantity of biscuit, and some butter —which were all willingly accepted.

Our messenger made a speech unto him [the Indian king]: That King James [of England] saluted him with words of love and peace; and did accept of him as his friend and ally; and that our governor desired to see him and to truck [or trade for animal furs]

---

1   Cornhill oddly recurs. The Pilgrims dubbed an Indian site Corn Hill, and, unbeknown to them, their agents published their report in Cornhill, London.
2   The 1622 text is "a jewel *at it*," misprinting *att.,* an abbreviation of *attached*.

with him; and to confirm a peace with him, as his next neighbor. He [the Indian king] liked well of the speech and heard it attentively, though the interpreters did not well express it.

After he [the king] had eaten and drunk himself [of our gifts of food], and given the rest to his company, he looked upon our messenger's sword and armor which he had on, with intimation of his desire to buy it. But on the other side, our messenger [Edward Winslow] showed his unwillingness to part with it.

In the end, he [the Indian king] left him [our messenger] in the custody of *Quadequina*, his brother. And [the king] came over the brook, and some twenty men following him, leaving all their bows and arrows behind them.

We kept six or seven [Indians] as hostages for our messenger [and his safety]. Captain Standish and Master *Williamson [Issac Allerton]*[1] met the Indian king at the brook, with half a dozen musketeers [in full armor with their guns]. They saluted him; and he, them.

So [three of our men served as an honor guard or escort for the king]—one going over [behind him], the [second] one on the one side, and the other [third musketeer] on the other. [They] conducted him to an house then in-building [or under construction], where we placed a green rug and three or four cushions. Then instantly came our governor [John Carver] with drum and trumpet after him, and some few musketeers [as his escort]. After salutations [and] our governor kissing his hand, the Indian king kissed him.

And so they sat down. The governor called for some strong water [mixed with liquor] and drunk to him. And he [the Indian king] drunk a great draft that made him sweat all the while after.

---

1 *Issac Allerton* was the husband of Mary Allerton, who died a few weeks earlier. The 1622 book misprints the name as *Williamson;* no such person exists.

[Peace Treaty with Massasoit]

He [Governor Carver] called for a little fresh meat, which the king did eat willingly and did give his followers. Then they treated of peace [and made an agreement], which was:

1. That neither he [the Indian king] nor any of his [people] should injure or do hurt to any of our people.
2. And if any of his did hurt to any of ours, he should send the offender, that we might punish him.
3. That if any of our tools were taken away when our people were at work, he should cause them to be restored; and if ours did any harm to any of his, we would do the like to them.
4. If any[one] did unjustly war against him, we would aid him. If any did war against us, he should aid us.
5. He should send [notice] to his neighbor[ing] confederates, to certify them of this, that they might not wrong us, but might be likewise comprised in the conditions of peace.
6. That when their men came to us, they should leave their bows and arrows behind them as we should do our [gun]-pieces when we came to them.

> The agreements of peace between us and Massasoit.

Lastly, that doing thus, King James[1] would esteem of him as his friend and ally—all which the [Indian] king seemed to like well, and it was applauded of his followers. [But] all the while he sat by the governor, he [the Indian king] trembled for fear.

[Strong Men]

In his person, he [the Indian king] is a very *lusty [vigorous]* man, in his best years—an able body, grave of countenance, and spare of speech. In his attire, little or nothing [was] differing from the rest of his followers [except] only in a great chain of white bone beads about his neck. And attached[2] behind his neck, hangs a little bag of tobacco which he *drank* and gave us to *drink*.[3]

---

1 King James I (1566-1625) ruled England 1603-1625.
2 The 1622 text is *"at it,"* misprinting *att.*, an abbreviation for *attached*.
3 A medieval idiom; to *drink* tobacco was to smoke it.

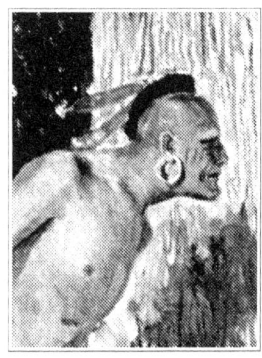
His face was painted with a sad red, like *murrey [dark mulberry-red]*. And [he] oiled both head and face [so] that he looked greasily. All his followers likewise were in their faces, in part or in whole, painted. Some [were] black, some red, some yellow, and some white—some with crosses and other antic works. Some had skins [or furs of animals] on them, and some [were] naked. All [were] strong, tall—all men in appearance.

So after all was done, the governor conducted him [the Indian king] to the brook. And there they embraced each other, and he departed—we diligently keeping our hostages [until our man, Edward Winslow, returned]. We expected our messenger's coming, but, anon, word was brought us that *Quadequina* [the king's brother] was coming, and our messenger was stayed till his return.

[King Massasoit's Brother]

[We quickly prepared for the king's brother] who presently came, and a troupe [of Indians] with him. So likewise [as before with the king], we entertained him [the brother] and conveyed him to the place prepared. He was very fearful of our [gun]-pieces and made signs of dislike that they should be carried away, whereupon commandment was given, they should be laid away.

He [the king's brother] was a very proper, tall young man of a very modest and *seemly countenance [handsome appearance]*. And he did kindly like of our entertainment [of food and drink]. So we conveyed him likewise as we did the king, but diverse of their people stayed [with us] still when he was returned. Then they dismissed our messenger [Edward Winslow, who returned to us].

[Yet, some of the king's Indians remained with us.] Two of his people would have stayed all night, but we would not suffer it— [we did not permit them to stay].

One thing I forgot—the king had in his bosom, hanging in a string, a great long knife. He [also] marveled much at our trumpet, and some of his men would sound [or play] it as well as they could.

[As for] *Samoset* and *Squanto*, they stayed all night with us. And the king and all his men lay all night in the woods not above half an English mile from us, and all their wives and women with them.

[New Neighbors]

They said that within eight or nine days, they would come and set corn on the other side of the brook *[now called Town Brook]* and dwell there all summer, which is hard-by us [or directly next to our colony]. That night, we kept good watch [with armed guards around camp], but there was no appearance of danger.

The next morning, diverse of their people came over to us, hoping to get some victuals, as we imagined. Some of them told us the king would have some of us come see him.

Captain Standish and Isaac *Alderton [Allerton]*[1] went venturously, who were welcomed of him [by the king *Massasoit*], after their manner. He gave them three or four groundnuts and some tobacco.

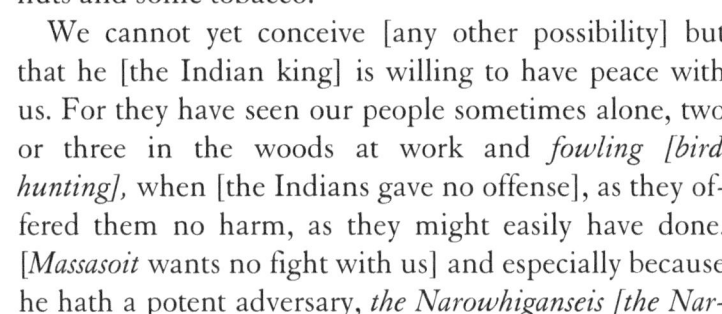

We cannot yet conceive [any other possibility] but that he [the Indian king] is willing to have peace with us. For they have seen our people sometimes alone, two or three in the woods at work and *fowling [bird hunting]*, when [the Indians gave no offense], as they offered them no harm, as they might easily have done. [*Massasoit* wants no fight with us] and especially because he hath a potent adversary, *the Narowhiganseis [the Narragansett Indians of western Rhode Island]*, that are at war with him (against whom, he thinks, we may be some strength to him, for our [gun]-pieces are terrible unto them).

This morning, they stayed till ten or eleven of the clock. And our governor bid them, "Send the king's kettle," and filled it full of peas, which pleased them well. And so they went their way.

---

1 Issac *Allerton* was a friend of Edward Winslow, an author of this report.

Friday [the 23rd of March 1621] was a very fair day. *Samoset* and *Squanto* still remained with us.

Squanto [who was also called *Tisquantum*] went at noon to fish for eels. At night, he came home with as many as he could well lift in one hand, which our people were glad of. They [the eels] were fat and sweet. He trod them out [of a creek bottom] with his feet and so caught them with his hands, without any other instrument.

This day [the 23rd of March] we proceeded on with our common business, from which we had been so often hindered by the *salvages* coming. And [we] concluded both of military orders and of some laws and orders as we thought behooveful *[sic]* for our present estate and condition.

And [we] did likewise choose our governor for this [coming] year [1621-1622], which was Master John Carver, a man well approved amongst us.[1]

---

1 The Pilgrims are here reelecting John Carver (1576-1621) as governor. He was an early organizer of the *Mayflower* expedition and was confirmed as governor on November 11, 1620, as part of the formalities related to the Mayflower Compact. Four months later, on March 23, 1621, the Pilgrims again chose Mr. Carver as governor for the coming year, which then began on March 25, not January 1. However, two weeks later, on April 5, 1621, Governor Carver suffered a massive stroke and died shortly thereafter. The Pilgrims elected William Bradford, an author of this report, to succeed him.

[Episode I – Pokanoket]

A
JOURNEY TO *POKANOKET*,[1]
[the Kingdom of the Wampanoag Indians]
The Habitation of the Great King **Massasoit**.
As also our Message, the Answer [from the King]
and *Entertainment [Hospitality]*
we had of
HIM.

It seemed good to the company [of our people], for many considerations, to send some [delegates from] amongst them to *Massasoit*, the greatest commander amongst the savages, bordering about us *[in a land called Pokanoket, which was southwest of Plymouth and included parts of present-day Massachusetts and Rhode Island]*. [Our reasons for sending delegates were] partly to know where to find them [the *Wampanoag* or *Pokanoket* Indians of *Massasoit*] if occasion served; as also to see their strength; discover the country; prevent abuses in their disorderly coming unto us; [and] make satisfaction for some conceived injuries [*viz.*, corn we took].

[We also wanted *Massasoit* to deliver an offer of repayment] to be done on our parts [making amends to the Indian owners of the taken corn]; and to continue the league of peace and friendship between them [*Massasoit's* tribe] and us.

For these and the like ends, it pleased the governor [William Bradford][2] to make choice of Steven Hopkins and Edward Winslow to go unto him [the Indian king] and [negotiate for us]. [We also sent an interpreter], having a fit opportunity by reason of a savage called *Tisquantum* (that could speak English) coming unto us. Withal [the] expedition [was] provided a horseman's coat of red cotton—and laced with a slight lace—for a present. [This was so] that both they [our men] and their message might be the more acceptable amongst them [the Indians].

---

1 The updated term, *Pokanoket,* replaces the Pilgrims' spelling of *Packanokik* and *Pakanokick* in this section.
2 William Bradford succeeded John Carver. See footnote on previous page.

The message was as followeth:

- That for as much as his subjects came often and without fear upon all occasions amongst us, so we were now come unto him [the Indian king]. And, in witness of the love and goodwill the English bear unto him, the governor hath sent him a coat, desiring that the peace and amity that was between them and us might be continued.
- [Our reason for coming was] not that we feared them, but because we intended not to injure any, desiring to live peaceably. And as with all men, so especially [we wish peace] with them, our nearest neighbors.
- But whereas his people came very often and very many together unto us—bringing, for the most part, their wives and children with them—they were welcome. Yet, we being but strangers as yet at *Patuxet*, alias New Plymouth, and not knowing how our corn might prosper [at our first harvest], we could no longer give them such entertainment as we had done—and as we desired still to do.
- Yet, if he would be pleased to come himself—or any special friend of his desired to see us—coming from him, they should be welcome. And to the end [of recognizing his friends, so that] we might know them from others, our governor had sent him a copper chain, desiring if any messenger should come from him to us, we might know him by bringing it with him; and [we would] hearken and give credit to his message accordingly.
- Also, requesting him that such as have skins [or furs of animals to trade] should bring them to us; and that he would hinder the multitude from [too often] oppressing us with them.
- And whereas, at our first arrival at *Paomet [or Pamet River]* (called by us Cape Cod), we found there corn buried in the ground—and finding no inhabitants but some graves of [the] dead, new-buried —[we] took the corn, resolving if ever we could hear of any that had right thereunto, to make satisfaction to the full for it ...
    - Yet, since we understand the owners thereof were fled for fear of us, our desire was either to pay them with the like quantity of corn, English meal, or any other commodities we had to pleasure them withal. [We were] requesting him [the Indian king] that someone of his men might signify so much unto them [the Indian owners of the taken corn], and we would content him for his pains—[compensate him for his efforts].

- And last of all, our governor requested one favor of him, which was that he would exchange some of their corn for seed with us [so] that we might make trial which [type of corn] best agreed with the soil where we live.

[Trek to King Massasoit]

With these presents and message, we set forward [the 2nd of July 1621][1] about nine o'clock in the morning, our guide resolving that night to rest at *Nemasket [present-day Middleborough, Massachusetts]*, a town under *Massasoit* and conceived by us to be very near (because the inhabitants flocked so thick upon every slight occasion amongst us) but we found it to be some fifteen English miles.

On the way [to *Nemasket*], we found some ten or twelve men, women, and children which had pestered us till we were weary of them. [We were] perceiving that—as the [usual] manner of them, all is—where victual is easiest to be got, there they live, especially in the summer. By reason whereof, our bay affording many lobsters, they resort every springtide thither and now returned with us to *Nemasket*.

Thither we came [to *Nemasket*] about three o'clock afternoon, the inhabitants entertaining us with joy in the best manner they could, giving us a kind of bread called by them *maizium* [or cornbread] and the spawn [or roe] of shads, which then they got in abundance in so much as they gave us spoons to eat them. With these, they boiled musty acorns, but of the shads' [roe or fish eggs] we eat heartily.

After this, they desired one of our men to shoot at a crow, complaining what damage they sustained in their corn by them. [One of us fired his gun]—who [succeeded in] *shooting*[2] some *fourscore [eighty birds]* off and killing [some others]. They [the Indians] much admired it, as other shots on other occasions.

After this, *Tisquantum* [also called *Squanto*] told us we should hardly [at our slow pace] in one day, reach [the capital of] *Pokanoket*[3] *[the Indian village of Sowams, near modern Warren, Rhode*

---

1 The 1622 book erroneously prints the date as June 10, 1621.
2 *Shooing* away eighty birds seems more plausible than *shooting* eighty times.
3 *Pokanoket* was a large area in modern Rhode Island and Massachusetts, but the Pilgrims seem here only to be referring to a village.

Island on the approaches to Narragansett Bay]. [We agreed], moving us to go some eight miles further, where we should find more store [of supplies] and better victuals than there.

Being willing to hasten our journey, we went [to that farther place] and came thither at sunsetting, where we found many of the *Namascheucks* (they so calling the men of *Nemasket*) fishing upon a weir [or dam] which they had made on a river *[the Taunton River]* which belonged to them [and] where they caught abundance of bass *[in an area called Titicut, now part of Middleborough]*.

These [Indians] welcomed us also [and] gave us of their fish, and we, them of our victuals, not doubting but we should have enough *where ere we came[1]—[as before we came on our journey]*. There we lodged in the open fields [because] for houses, they had none (though they spent the most of the summer there).

The head of this river *[the Taunton River]* is reported to be not far from the place of our abode [at Plymouth]. Upon it are and have been many towns [of the Indians]—it being a good length.

The ground is very good on both sides [of the river], it being for the most part cleared. Thousands of men have lived there (which died in a great plague not long since). And pity it was—and is—to see so many goodly fields, and so well seated, without men to dress and manure the same—[no one to farm and fertilize the fields].

Upon this river, dwelleth *Massasoit* [in a village called *Sowams*]. It *[the Taunton River]* cometh into the sea at the *Narrohiganset Bay [Narragansett Bay in Rhode Island]*, where *[sic]* the Frenchmen so much use. A ship [large enough to sail the sea] may go many miles up it, as the *salvages* report, and a shallop to the head of it. But so far as we saw, we are [only] sure a shallop may [go upstream].

[Old Warriors]

But to return to our journey, the next morning we *break our fast [ate breakfast]*, took our leave, and departed, being then accompanied with some six *salvages* [serving as Indian guides]. Having gone about six miles by the riverside, [we came] at a known shoal place [to cross]. It being low water, they spake to us to put oft our breeches, for we must wade thorough *[sic]*.

---

1 Quaint idiom or misprint from 1622; "*wherever* we came" seems better.

Here, let me not forget the valor and courage of some of the *salvages* on the opposite side of the river. For there were remaining alive only two men, both aged, especially the one being above threescore *[sixty-years old]*. These two [were very brave]. Espying a company of men entering the river, [they] ran very swiftly and low in the grass to meet us at the bank, where, with shrill voices and great courage standing, [they] charged upon us with their bows.

They demanded what [and who] we were, supposing us to be enemies and thinking to take advantage on us in the water. But seeing we were friends, they welcomed us with such food as they had. And we bestowed a small bracelet of beads on them.

Thus far, we are sure the [sea] tide ebbs and flows ... [?][1]

[A Plentiful Country]

Having here again refreshed ourselves, we proceeded in our journey, the weather being very hot for travel. Yet, the country [was] so well-watered that a man could scarce be dry but he should have a spring at hand to cool his thirst—beside [or besides] small rivers in abundance. But the *salvages* will not willingly drink but at a spring head.

When we came to any small brook where no bridge was, two of them [of the six Indians guides] desired to carry us through, of

---

1 A misprinted sentence from 1622. It is too vague to restore.

their own accords. Also, fearing we were or would be weary, [they] offered to carry our [gun]-pieces. Also, if we would lay off any of our clothes, we should have them carried.

And as the one of them [of the six Indian guides] had found more special kindness from one of the messengers [of Plymouth]—and the other *salvage* [was treated well] from the other [of our men]—so they [the Indians] showed their thankfulness accordingly in affording us all help and furtherance in the journey.

As we passed along, we observed that there were few places by the river [with homes now], but [the area] had been inhabited [in the past by the Indians]. [We knew this] by reason whereof much ground was clear [of trees and shrubs], save of weeds which grew higher than our heads.

There is much good timber, both *[sic]* oak, walnut tree, fir, beech, and exceeding great chestnut trees. The country, in respect of [the terrain]—the lying of it—is both *champaigny [open plains]* and hilly, like many places in England.

In some places, it's very rocky, both above ground and in it. And though the country be wild and overgrown with woods—yet, the trees stand not thick, but [rather] a man may well ride a horse amongst them.

[A Stranger]

Passing on at length, one of the company [of people with us], an Indian, espied a man and told the rest of it. We asked them if they feared any[one]. They told us that if they were *Narrohigganset men [Narragansett Indians]*, they would not trust them.

Whereat, we called for our [gun]-pieces and bid them not to fear. For though they were twenty, we two [delegates from Plymouth] alone would not care for them—[we were not afraid to fight them].

But, they hailing him [the stranger], he proved a friend and had only two women with him. Their baskets were empty, but they fetched water in their bottles so that we drank with them and departed.

After[wards], we met another man with [an]other two women which had been at rendezvous [or camped] by the salt water. And their baskets were full of roasted crab-fishes and other dried shell-fish, of which they gave us. And we eat *[sic]* and drank with them. And [we] gave each of the women a string of beads and departed.

[An Indian Town]

After[wards], we came to a town of *Massasoit's [Mattapoiset or Gardners Neck in present-day Swansea, Massachusetts]* where we eat oysters and other fish. From thence, we went to [the capital of] *Pokanoket [the village of Sowams, near Warren, Rhode Island]*. But

Massasoit was not at home. [Yet] there we stayed, he being sent for. When news was brought of his coming, our guide, *Tisquantum,* requested that at our meeting, we would discharge our [gun]-pieces. But [when] one of us [was] going about to charge his piece [with gunpowder and bullets], the women and children, through fear to see him take up his piece, ran away. And [they] could not be pacified till he laid it down again. [The people thus quieted] who afterward were better informed by our interpreter.

[Meeting Massasoit]

Massasoit being come, we discharged our [gun]-pieces and saluted him, who, after their manner, kindly welcomed us. And [he] took us into his house and set us down by him. [**Editor's Note: By an odd coincidence, this first meeting in the home of an Indian king occurred on July 4, 1621, the first Fourth of July in America for the Pilgrims. The Fourth of July was, of course, destined to be a momentous holiday for their descendants—Independence Day from their English persecutors.**]

[This was] where [we] having delivered our foresaid message and presents—and having put the coat on his back and the chain about his neck—he [the king] was not a little proud to behold himself. And his men also [delighted] to see their king so bravely attired.

For [his] answer to our message, he told us we were welcome, and he would gladly continue that peace and friendship which was between him and us. And for his men, they should no more pester us, as they had done. Also, [he agreed] that he would send [a messenger for us] to *Paomet [the Pamet River in Truro on Cape Cod]*[1] and would help us with corn for seed, according to our request.

This being done, his men gathered near to him—to whom he turned himself and made a great speech, they sometime interposing and, as it were, confirming and applauding him in that [which] he said. The meaning whereof was (as far as we could learn) thus:

> "Was not he, *Massasoit,* Commander of the Country about them? Was not such a town his [to rule], and the people of it? And should they not bring their skins [and furs of animals] unto us [for trade]?"

---

1 In November 1620, the Pilgrims took corn from unknown Indians on Cape Cod. *Massosoit's* messenger delivers an offer of repayment from the Pilgrims.

To which they answered, they were his [to rule] and would be at peace with us—and bring their skins [and furs of animals] to us. After this manner, he named at least thirty places [that the king ruled], and their answer was as aforesaid to every one [of these places too]. So that as it was delightful, it was tedious unto us.

This being ended, he lighted tobacco for us and fell to discoursing of England and of the King's Majesty, marveling that he [King James] would live without a wife.[1] Also, he talked of the Frenchmen, bidding us not to *suffer [permit]* them to come to *Narrohiganset [Narragansett Bay]*, for it was King James's—his country; and he *[Massasoit]* also was King James's—his man.

[Sleeping with the King]

Late it grew, but victuals he offered none. For indeed, he had not any, being he came so newly home. So we desired to go to rest. He laid us on the bed with himself and his wife, they at the one end, and we [two delegates from Plymouth] at the other—it being only planks laid a foot from the ground, and a thin mat upon them.

Two more of his chief men [slept next to us]. For want of room, [they] pressed by and upon us, so that we were worse weary of our lodging than of our journey.

The next day being Thursday [the 5th of July 1621], many of their *sachmis,* or petty governors, came to see us, and many of their men also. There they went to their manner of games for skins [and furs of animals] and knives.

There we challenged them to shoot with them for skins [and furs], but they durst not. Only they desired to see one of us shoot at a mark—[a target posted on a tree]. [One of us made a shot] who [surprised them by] shooting with *hail-shot [buckshot or smaller shotgun-like pellets];* they wondered to see the mark so full of holes.

About one o'clock, *Massasoit* brought two fishes that he had shot [with an arrow or spear]. They were like *bream [catfish or bass]* but three times so big and better meat. These being boiled, there were at least forty [of the Indians who] looked for share in them, [and] the most [of these people did] eat of them. This meal [was the]

---

1   The wife of King James I of England died in 1619.

only we had in two nights and a day. And had not one of us bought a partridge [from an Indian], we had taken our journey fasting [or without food].

Very importunate, he [the king] was to have us stay with them longer. But we desired to keep the Sabbath at home [that Sunday] and feared we should either be light-headed for want of sleep [or too weak to make the long journey home]. For what with bad lodging, the savages' barbarous singing (for they use to sing themselves asleep), lice and fleas within doors, and mosquitoes *without [outdoors]*—we could hardly sleep all the time of our being there.

Indian King, Virginia, 1607

We [were] much fearing that if we should stay any longer, we should not be able to recover home for want of strength. So that on the Friday morning [the 6th of July 1621] before sunrising, we took our leave and departed. *Massasoit* [was sorry to see us go], being both grieved and ashamed that he could no better entertain us.

And [the king satisfied us by] retaining *Tisquantum* [our interpreter] to send from place to place to procure *truck for us—[a regular trade in animal furs or skins]*—and appointing another [new interpreter] called *Tokamahamon* in his place, whom we had found faithful, before and after[wards], upon all occasions.

[The Journey Home]

At this town of *Massasoit's [Mattapoiset or Gardners Neck in present-day Swansea, Massachusetts]* where we before [stopped to] eat, we were again refreshed with a little fish. And [we] bought about a handful of meal of their parched corn, which was very precious at that time of the year, and a small string of dried shellfish as big as oysters. The latter we gave to the six savages that accompanied us [as Indian guides], keeping the [corn] meal for ourselves. When we drank [water], we eat *[sic]* each a spoonful of it (with a pipe of tobacco) instead of other victuals. And of this [tobacco] also, we could not but give them [a share] so long as it lasted.

[After walking] five miles, they led us to a house, out of the way, in hope of victuals. But we found nobody there and so were but worse able to return home [having wasted effort going to the house]. That night we reached to the weir *[the fishing-dam on the Taunton River]* where we lay before, but the *Namascheucks* were returned [to their village], so that we had no hope of anything [to eat] there.

[With an arrow or spear] one of the savages [or Indian guides] had shot a shad in the water and [also got] a small squirrel as big as a rat, called a *neuxis*. The one half of either he gave us and after[wards] went to the weir to fish. From hence, we wrote to Plymouth and sent *Tokamahamon* [with our note] before to *Nemasket*, willing him from thence to send another [fresh runner to relay it to Plymouth], [so] that he might meet us with food at *Nemasket*.

Two men [of the original six Indian guides] now only remained with us, and it pleased God to give them good store of fish [from the river], so that we were well-refreshed. After supper, we [the delegates from Plymouth] went to rest, and they [the Indians], to fishing again. More [fish] they *gat*[1] and fell to eating afresh—and retained sufficient ready-roast [fish] for all our breakfasts.

[On Saturday, the 7th of July 1621], about two o'clock in the morning, [there] arose a great storm of wind, rain, lightning, and thunder—in such violent manner that we could not keep in our fire. And had the savages not roasted fish when we were asleep, we had set forward fasting [without food on the final leg of our journey back to Plymouth]. For the rain still continued with great violence, even the whole day through, till we came within two miles of home.

Being wet and weary, at length we came to *Nemasket [present-day Middleborough, Massachusetts, fifteen miles southwest of Plymouth]*. There we refreshed our-

---

1   *Gat* is a medieval form of *got*; some regions still use *gat* in vernacular speech.

selves, giving gifts to all such [Indians] as had showed us any kindness. [Yet] amongst others, [we ignored] one of the six that came with us from [the Indian kingdom of] *Pokanoket*—[this particular person] having before this, on the way, unkindly forsaken us.

[This Indian] marveled [when] we gave him nothing and told us what he had done for us. We also told him of some discourtesies he offered us, whereby he deserved nothing.

Yet, we gave him a small trifle, whereupon he offered us tobacco. But the house being full of [Indian] people, we told them he stole some by the way. And if it were of that, we would not take it. For we would not receive that which was stolen, upon any terms. If we did, our God would be angry with us and destroy us.

This abashed him and gave the rest [of the Indians] great content. But at our departure, he would, [if] needs [be so], carry him [one of our delegates from Plymouth] on his back through a river. [The Indian helped the same man] whom he had formerly, in some sort, abused.

Fain [happily] they [the Indians] would have had us to lodge there [at *Nemasket*] all night, and wondered [why] we would set forth again in such weather. But God be praised, we came safe home that night, though wet, weary, and *surbated [exhausted by travel]*.

[Episode II – Nauset]

A
VOYAGE MADE BY TEN
of our Men to the Kingdom of
NAUSET *[eastern Cape Cod]* to seek a Boy that had
lost himself in the[1] WOODS;
[Told] with such Accidents as
the befell us in that
VOYAGE.

[Editor's Note: In late July of 1621, the Pilgrims sent explorers about thirty miles to the southeast, going by sailboat along the coastline of Cape Cod Bay. They went to recover a lost child of theirs, John Billington, Jr.,[2] who had been found, transferred, and held by a series of mysterious Indians. The Pilgrims knowingly risked life and limb to recover the boy; among the natives holding the boy were those who had attacked the Pilgrims on Cape Cod in the First Encounter of December 1620.]

The [end of July 1621][3] we set forth [into the Bay of Cape Cod], the weather being very fair. But ere we had been long at sea—[shortly after we sailed into the bay]—there arose a storm of wind and rain with much lightning and thunder, in so much that a spout [of storm-tossed water] arose not far from us.

But God be praised, it [en]dured not long, and we put in that night for harbor at a place called *Cummaquid [present-day Barnstable Harbor, thirty miles southeast of Plymouth]*, where we had some hope to find the boy. Two savages [who were our friends] were in the boat with us: the one was *Tisquantum* [also called *Squanto*], our interpreter; the other, *Tokamahamon,* a special friend.

It being night before we came in *[at Barnstable Harbor]*, we anchored in the middest of the bay where we were dry at a low

---

1 Original italics.
2 John Billington, Jr., was the older brother of Francis Billington, who nearly blew up the *Mayflower* in December 1620. The family continued its mishaps; in 1630, the Pilgrims hung the father of the two boys for murder.
3 The 1622 text misprints the date as "*11th of June.*" William Bradford, one of the Pilgrim authors, later dated the event as between the end of July and the 13th of August 1621. See Henry Martyn Dexter, editor, *Mourt's Relation* (Boston: John Kimball Wiggin, 1865) footnote 365, page 112.

[tide]water. In the morning, we espied savages seeking lobsters [in the shallows of the harbor] and sent our two interpreters [wading over] to speak with them, the channel [of water] being between them [and serving as a moat or natural defense].¹

[This was] where they told them what we were, and for what we were come, willing [or urging] them not at all to fear us, for we would not hurt them. Their answer was that the boy was well, but he was at *Nauset [about twenty miles to the East at present-day Eastham, Massachusetts on the bay shore of Cape Cod].*

Yet, since we were there, they desired us to come ashore and eat with them, which, as soon as our boat floated [with the tide], we did. And [thus] went six [of our men] ashore, having [exchanged] four pledges [of Indians as hostages] for them in the boat.

[Governor Iyanough*]*

They brought us to their *sachem* or governor, whom they call *Iyanough,* a man not exceeding twenty-six years of age, but very personable, gentle, courteous, and fair conditioned. Indeed [he was] not like a savage, save for his attire. His entertainment was answerable to his parts—[his hospitality matched his fine character]—and his cheer [was] plentiful and various.

One thing was very grievous unto us at this place. There was an old woman, whom we judged to be no less than an hundred years old, which came to see us because she never saw English[men]. Yet [she] could not behold us without breaking forth into great passion, weeping, and crying excessively. We demanding the reason of it,

---

1   At low tide, channels of seawater form on bottoms of shallow harbors.

they told us. She had three sons, who, when Master Hunt [the English sea captain] was in these parts, went aboard his ship to trade with him. And he carried them [as] captives into Spain (for *Tisquantum* at that time was carried away also) by which means, she was deprived of the comfort of her children in her old age.

We told them we were sorry that any Englishman should give them that offense, that Hunt was a bad man, and that all the English that heard of it, condemned him for the same. But for us, we would not offer them any such injury, though it would gain us all the skins [or furs of animals] in the country. So we gave her some small trifles, which somewhat appeased her.

After dinner, we took boat for *Nauset [heading for Eastham on Cape Cod]*, *Iyanough* and two of his men accompanying us. Ere [or before] we came to *Nauset*, the day and tide were almost spent, in so much as we could not go in with our shallop [the sea being too low to float the boat over flat sands near shore]. But *[Iyanough]*, the *sachem* or governor of *Commaquid*, went ashore [by wading to the beach], and his men with him. We also sent *Tisquantum* to tell *Aspinet*, the *sachem* of *Nauset*, wherefore we came.

[Later] the savages here came very thick amongst us and were earnest with us to bring in our boat [to shore to meet them]. But

we neither well could [because of the low tide] nor yet desired to do it because we had least cause to trust them, being they only had formerly made an assault upon us in the same place.

[In December of 1620, they ambushed us] in [the] time of our winter discovery for [a place of] habitation. And indeed it was no marvel they did so. For howsoever, through snow or otherwise, we saw no houses [at that time]— yet we were in the middest of them [frightening their people].

[Owner of Corn]

[On our present visit], when our boat was aground *[near the mouth of the present-day Herring River in Eastham]*, they [the Indians] came very thick. But we stood therein, upon our guard, not suffering any to enter [our boat], except two, the one being of *Maramoick [an Indian town at present-day Chatham, Massachusetts]*.

And [the other Indian was] one of those whose corn we had formerly found. We promised him restitution and desired him either to come to *Patuxet* [alias New Plymouth] for satisfaction, or else we would bring them so much corn again. He promised to come; we *used [hosted]* him very kindly for the present.

Some few skins [of animals] we gat there, but not many.

[King Aspinet*]*

After sunset, *Aspinet* [the local king of the Indians] came with a great train [of his people] and brought the boy with him, one bearing him through the water. He *[Aspinet]* had not less than an hundred [of his people] with him. The half whereof came to the shallop['s] side—unarmed—with him. The other [remaining half of his people] stood aloof, with their bow and arrows.

There *[at the Herring River in Eastham]* he delivered us the boy, behung with beads, and made peace with us—[we] bestowing [as a gift] a knife on him *[Aspinet]* and likewise on another that first entertained the boy and brought him thither. So they departed from us.

Here we understood [from the natives] that the *Narrohigansets [the Narragansett Indians of Rhode Island]* had spoiled [or killed] some of *Massasoit's* men and taken him [captive]. This struck some fear in us because the colony [at New Plymouth] was so weakly guarded—the strength thereof being abroad [on this journey].

But we set forth with resolution to make the best haste home we could. Yet, the wind being contrary, having scarce any fresh water left, and at least sixteen leagues home *[forty-eight miles to Plymouth],*[1] we put in again for the shore *[at Barnstable Harbor].*

There we met again with *Iyanough*, the *sachem* of *Cummaquid,* and the most of his town, both men women and children with him. He, being still willing to gratify us, took a rundlet [or small cask] and led our men—in the dark—a great way for water, but could find none good. Yet, [he] brought such [water from his town] as there was, [in a cask dangling from a strap] on his neck, with them.

In the meantime, the women joined hand in hand, singing and dancing before the shallop [our boat being moored just offshore in the harbor]. The men [were] also showing all the kindness they could, with *Iyanough* himself taking a bracelet from about his neck and hanging it upon one of us.

Again, we set out [to return home] but to small purpose. For we gat but little homeward [as we lacked wind for our sails]. Our water also was very brackish and not to be drunk.

The next morning, *Iyanough* espied us again [from the shore] and ran after us. We, being resolved to go to *Cummaquid* again to [fetch drinking] water, took him into the shallop. [We carried *Iyanough* back to his town] whose entertainment [of our needs] was not inferior unto the former [visit of ours].

The soil at *Nauset [eastern Cape Cod at Eastham]* and here *[central Cape Cod at Barnstable Harbor]*[2] is alike—even and sandy, not so good for corn as where we are [at New Plymouth]. Ships may safely ride in either harbor. In the summer, they [the harbors] abound with fish.

Being now watered, we put forth again and, by God's Providence, came safely home that night [sometime before the 13th of August 1621].

---

1 The straight-line distance is about 30 miles.
2 Modern Cape Cod refers to the entire hooked peninsula extending from the mainland of Massachusetts to Provincetown. The Pilgrims, though, may have deemed Cape Cod to be only the eastern end from Eastham to Provincetown.

[Episode III – Nemasket][1]

A
JOURNEY TO THE
Kingdom of *NEMASKET*
in defense of the Great King
Massasoit against the
Narrohiggansets [the Narragansett Indians],
and to revenge
the supposed Death
of our Interpreter
Tisquantum [also called *Squanto*].

At our return from *Nauset [eastern Cape Cod]*, we found it true that *Massasoit* was put from his country by the *Narrohiggansets [the Narragansett Indians of Rhode Island]*.[2] Word also was brought unto us that one *Corbitant*,[3] a petty *sachem* or governor under *Massasoit*—[and] whom they ever feared to be too conversant with the *Narragansetts*—was at *Nemasket [present-day Middleborough, Massachusetts, fifteen miles southwest of Plymouth]*.

[We were concerned about *Corbitant*] who fought to draw the hearts of *Massasoit's* subjects from him. [*Corbitant* was] speaking also disdainfully of us, storming at the peace between [the Indians of] *Nauset, Cummaquid,* and us. And [*Corbitant* was angry] at *Tisquantum,* [who was] the worker of it [*Tisquantum* being our interpreter and negotiator of the peace treaties].

Also [Corbitant railed] at *Tokamahamon* and one *Hobbamock,* two Indians, our allies[4]—one of which [?],[5] he would treacherously have murdered a little before [when many of us were away on Cape Cod], [the would-be victim] being a special and trusty man of *Massasoit's*.

[We became involved when our friend] *Tokamahamon* went to him [meeting *Corbitant* at *Nemasket*], but the other two, *Tisquan-*

---
1 *Nemasket* replaces the 1622 spelling of *Namaschet*.
2 Hereafter, only the modern spelling, *Narragansett[s]*, is used.
3 *Corbitant* replaces *Coubatant* in the 1622 text.
4 Rather than *our allies*, the 1622 text is *or Lemes*, a misprint.
5 Both *Tokamahamon* and *Hobbamock* were in danger, but only the threat to *Hobbamock* is later described in detail.

tum and *Hobbamock*, would not. Yet [they] put their lives in their hands [and] privately went to see if they could hear of their king [*Massasoit*, being held captive]. And lodging at *Nemasket*, [they] were discovered to *Corbitant*, who set a guard to beset the house and took *Tisquantum* [as prisoner]. For he [*Corbitant*] had said if he [our interpreter] were dead, the English had lost their tongue.

Hobbamock [was frightened], seeing that *Tisquantum* was taken, and *Corbitant* held a knife at his breast. [And] being a strong and stout man [*Hobbamock* ran away and did] break from them and came to New Plymouth, full of fear and sorrow for *Tisquantum*, whom he thought to be slain.

Upon this news, the company [of our people] assembled together and resolved, on the morrow, to send ten men armed [with guns] to *Nemasket*. And [they appointed] *Hobbamock* for their guide—to revenge the supposed death of *Tisquantum* on *Corbitant*, our bitter enemy.

And [our men were] to [seize and] retain *Nepeof,* another *sachem* or governor who was of this confederacy, till we heard what was become of our friend, *Massasoit*.

[Assault on Nemasket*]*

On the morrow [Tuesday, 14th of August 1621], we set out ten men armed [with guns], who took their journey, as aforesaid. But the day proved very wet. When we supposed we were within three or four miles of *Nemasket,* we went out of the way, [hid ourselves], and stayed there till night because we would not be discovered.

There we consulted what to do, [delaying] and thinking best to beset the house at midnight. Each was appointed his task by the captain [of our militia, Miles Standish], all men encouraging one another to the utmost of their power. [However], by night our guide lost his way, which much discouraged our men, being we were wet and weary of our [fire]arms [and armor]. But one of our men, having been before at *Nemasket,* brought us into the way again.

Before we came to the town, we sat down and ate such as our knapsack afforded. That being done, we threw them aside—and all such things as might hinder us—and so went on and beset the house [where *Corbitant* might be], according to our last resolution.

Those [of us] that entered [the house] demanded if *Corbitant* were not there, but fear had bereft the savages of speech. We *charged [ordered]* them not to stir, for if *Corbitant* were not there, we would not meddle with them. If he were [in the house], we came principally for him, [seeking] to be avenged on him for the supposed death of *Tisquantum*, and other matters. But, howsoever, we would not at all hurt their women or children.

Notwithstanding, some of them pressed out at a private door and escaped, but with some wounds. At length [though], perceiving our principal ends [some Indians helped us]. They told us *Corbitant* was returned *[to his home village of Mattapoiset or Gardners Neck in present-day Swansea, Massachusetts]* with all his train [of men], and that *Tisquantum* was yet living. And in the town [people were] offering some tobacco [and] other such as they had to eat.

[However], in this hurly-burly, we discharged two [gun]-pieces at random, which much terrified all the inhabitants—except *Tisquantum* and *Tokamahamon,* who, though they knew not our end [or purpose] in coming, yet assured them of our honesty, that we would not hurt them.

Those boys that were in the house, seeing our care of women, often cried, "*Neen squaes!*"—that is to say, "I am a woman." The women also [were] hanging upon *Hobbamock,* calling him "*Towam,*" that is, "Friend."

But to be short, we kept them [as prisoners] we had, and made them make a fire [so] that we might see to search the house. In the meantime, *Hobbamock* gat on the top of the house and called *Tisquantum* and *Tokamahamon*, which came unto us, accompanied with others, some armed and others naked.

Those that had bows and arrows, we took them away, promising [to return] them again when it was day. The house, we took [and sheltered there] for our better safeguard. But [we] released those we had taken, manifesting whom we came for and *wherefore [why]*.

On the next morning, we marched into the middest of the town and went to the house of *Tisquantum* to breakfast. Thither came all whose hearts were upright towards us, but all *Corbitant's* faction were fled away.

There, in the middest of them, we manifested again our intendment [to seek justice], assuring them that although *Corbitant* had now escaped us ... yet there was no place [that] should secure him and his, from us. [We would punish *Corbitant*] if he continued his threatening us—and provoking others against us—who had kindly entertained him and never intended evil towards him till he now so justly deserved it.

Moreover, if *Massasoit* did not return in safety from *Narragansett*, or if hereafter, he *[Corbitant]* should make any insurrection against him or offer violence to *Tisquantum, Hobbamock*, or any of *Massasoit's* subjects, we would revenge it upon him—to the overthrow of him and his.

As for those were wounded, we were sorry for it, though themselves procured it (in not staying in the house at our command). Yet, if they would return home with us, our surgeon should heal them. At this offer, one man and a woman that were wounded went home with us.

Tisquantum and many other known friends [were] accompanying us and offering all help that might be, by carriage of anything we had to ease us. So that by God's good Providence, we safely returned home [to New Plymouth on Wednesday, the 15th of August 1621] the morrow night after we set forth.

[Episode IV - Massachusetts]

A
RELATION [or Report] OF OUR
Voyage to the *MASSACHUSETTS*
[The Indians at Boston Bay]
and what happened there.

It seemed good to the company [of our people], in general, that [we visit those Indians north of us], though the *Massachusetts* had often threatened us (as we were informed). Yet, we should go amongst them, partly to see the country, partly to make peace with them, and partly to procure their truck [a regular and long-term trade in furs and skins of animals].

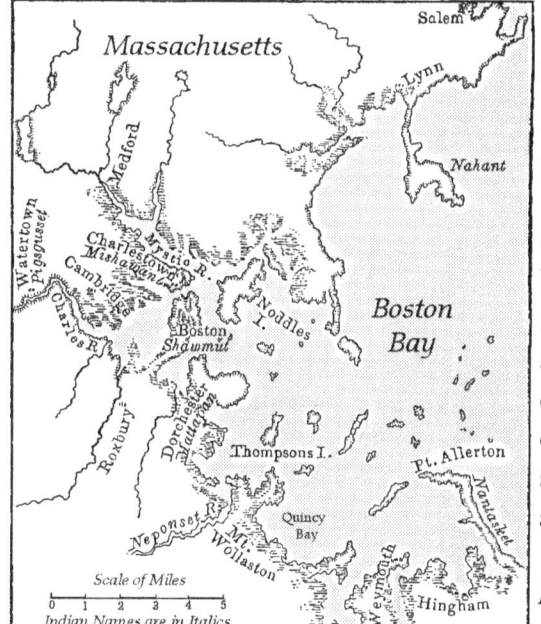

For these ends, the governors [of our Colony of New Plymouth] chose ten men fit for the purpose and sent *Tisquantum* [also called *Squanto*] and two other *salvages* to bring us to speech with the people and interpret for us.

We set out [*for Boston Bay*][1] about midnight [on the 18th of September 1621], the tide then serving for us [to float the shallop, our sailboat]. We, supposing it to be nearer than it is, thought to be there the next morning *betimes [early in the day]*. But it proved well near twenty leagues *[sixty miles]*[2] from New Plymouth *[to Boston Bay]*.

---
1 The bay was not formally named *Boston Bay* until after 1630, a decade later.
2 The straight-line distance, Plymouth to Boston, is closer to 40 miles. "Tacking," i.e., zig-zagging a sailboat against the wind, may explain the difference.

[Wednesday, the 19th of September 1621] – We came into the [southern] bottom of the bay *[at present-day Point Allerton]*, but, being late, we anchored and lay in the shallop, not having seen any of the people [who were the *Massachusetts* Indians]. The next morning, we put in for the shore *[near Quincy, Massachusetts]*. There we found many lobsters that had been gathered together by the *salvages* —[and] which we made ready under a cliff [storing the lobsters for the Indians until they returned].[1]

Boston Harbor, circa 1629

The captain [Miles Standish] set two sentinels[2] behind the cliff to the landward, to secure the shallop. And taking a guide [one of our Indian interpreters] with him, and four of our company, [he] went to seek the inhabitants, where *[sic]* they met a woman coming for her lobsters. They told her of them and contented her [not to fear] for them. She told them where the people [of her tribe] were.

Tisquantum went to [find] them. The rest [of our men] returned, having [lit a signal fire for] direction which way to bring the shallop to them [and pick them up along the shore of the bay].

[Governor Obbatinewat]

The *sachem*, or governor of this place, is called *Obbatinewat*. And though he live in the [south] bottom of the Massachusett[s] Bay, yet he is under [the rule of] *Massasoit [who lives far away in present-day Rhode Island]*. He *used [hosted]* us very kindly.

---

1   The Pilgrims are wary of handling Indian food. Ten months earlier, in November 1620, the settlers took native corn; combat and ill will followed.

2   "*Sent* two sentinels behind the cliff," seems more likely here.

He [the *sachem Obbatinewat*] told us he durst not then remain in any settled place, for fear of the *Tarentines [a tribe of Indians living along the Penobscot River in Maine]*. Also, the *Squa Sachem*, or *Massachusetts* Queen, was an enemy to him. We told him of diverse *sachems* [or Indian governors] that had acknowledged themselves to be King James's—his men [to rule and protect]. And if he *[Obbatinewat]* also would submit himself, we would be his safeguard from his enemies—which he did [accept] and went along with us to bring us to the *Squa Sachem*.

[Editor's Note: The Pilgrims used a variety of means to negotiate peace, including turning disadvantages into advantages. To impress the Indians at Boston Bay, they invoked the name of King James of England as their protector and friend. In reality, the English King was hostile to the Pilgrims, a key reason for their seeking refuge in America.]

Indian Ruler, Virginia, circa 1607

[The Northern Bay]

Again we crossed the bay *[present-day Boston Harbor]*, which is very large and hath at least fifty islands in it. (But the certain number [of islands] is not known to the inhabitants).

Night it was before we came to that [northern] side of the bay *[present-day Charlestown, Massachusetts]* where this people [the *Massachusetts* Indians] were [supposed to be living]. On shore, the *salvages* [who were our interpreters] went [searching] but found nobody. That night also, we rid *[sic]* at anchor aboard the shallop. On the morrow [Friday, the 21st of September 1621], we went ashore, all but two men, and marched *in arms [guns ready]* up in the country.

Having gone three miles, we came to a place where corn had been newly gathered, a house pulled down, and the people gone.

A mile from hence, *Nanepashemet*, their king in his lifetime, had lived. His house was not like others, but [rather] a scaffold was largely built with poles and planks some six foot from ground. And the house [was placed] upon that, being situated on the top of a hill *[later called Rock Hill in present-day Medford, Massachusetts]*.

Not far from hence, in a bottom [an area of low-lying land], we came to a fort *[near the Mystic Lakes in Medford]* built by their deceased king [in] the manner thus:

There were poles some thirty or forty-foot long, stuck in the ground as thick as they could be set, one by another. And with these, they enclosed a ring some forty or fifty foot over. A trench, breast-high, was digged on each side [to serve as a moat to defend the fort]. (One way there was to go into it with a bridge.) In the midst of this *palizada*[1] *[a circular wood fence],* stood the frame of an house wherein, [the king] being dead, he lay buried.

About a mile from hence, we came to such another [fort], but seated on the top of an hill. Here *Nanopashemet* was killed *[in 1619 by the Tarentine Indians of Maine],* none dwelling in it since the time of his death. At this place we stayed and sent two *salvages* [our Indian interpreters] to look [for] the inhabitants and to inform them of our ends in coming [so] that they might not be fearful of us.

Within a mile of this place, they found the women of the place, together with their corn on heaps. *Whither [to that place]* we supposed them to be fled for fear of us; and the more [we thought so] because in diverse places, they had newly pulled down their houses and, for haste, in one place had left some of their corn covered with a mat, and nobody with it.

With much fear, they entertained us at first [nervously hosting us as guests]. But seeing our gentle carriage towards them, they took heart and entertained us in the best manner they could, boiling cod and such other things as they had for us.

At length, with much sending for, came one of their men, shaking and trembling for fear. But when he saw we intended them no hurt but came to truck [or trade for skins and furs of animals], he

---

1 Spanish word, spelled *Pallizado* in the 1622 text.

promised us his skins [and furs] also. [Speaking further] of him, we inquired for their queen, but it seemed she was far from thence. At least, we could not see her.

Here, *Tisquantum* [also called *Squanto*] would have had us rifled the *salvage* women and taken their skins [of animals and furs], and all such things as might be serviceable for us. "For," said he, "they are a bad people and have oft threatened you."

But our answer was, "Were they never so bad? We would not wrong them or give them any just occasion against us."

For their words, we little weighed them. But if they once attempted anything against us, then we would deal far worse than he desired.

Having well spent the day, we returned to the shallop *[the sailboat being anchored in Boston Harbor at present-day Charlestown]*. Almost all the women [were] accompanying us to truck [or trade their furs for our beads, knives, or other items], [and] who sold their coats from their backs and tied boughs about them [to cover their nakedness]—but with great shamefacedness *[sic]*. (For indeed, they are more modest than some of our English women are.)

We promised them to come again to them; and they [promised] us to keep their skins [and furs of animals to sell to us].

[Great Boston Harbor]

Within this bay *[Boston Harbor]*, the *salvages* say there are two rivers *[the Mystic & Charles Rivers]*. The one whereof we saw, having a fair entrance *[probably the mouth of the Mystic River]*, but we had no time to discover it [in more detail].

Better harbors for shipping cannot be than here are [with good inlets, coves, and like shelters for ships and boats]. At the entrance of the bay are many rocks and, in all likelihood, very good fishing ground. Many, yea, most of the islands have been inhabited—some being cleared from end to end—but the people are all dead [from disease] or removed [themselves to new places].

Our victual[s] growing scarce, the wind coming fair, and having a light moon, we set out at evening [for New Plymouth]. And through the goodness of God, [we] came safely home before noon the day following [Saturday, the 22nd of September 1621].

[Appendix A – First Thanksgiving]

[Editor's Note: Edward Winslow, an author of this report, wrote the below letter, describing the First Thanksgiving in the autumn of 1621. He includes descriptions of plants and animals, as well as a "how-to" list for would-be immigrants to America. (This edition adds illustrations from the nineteenth century.)

The recipient of Mr. Winslow's letter may have been George Morton, an agent of the Pilgrims in London; Mr. Morton planned to sail later to America to join them. See Appendix D for more about Mr. Morton.]

A
LETTER SENT FROM
New England to a friend in these parts [of Old England],
setting forth a brief and true Declaration
of the worth of that Plantation in America;
As also certain useful Directions
for such as intend a VOYAGE
into those Parts [of the New World].

Loving and old friend: Although I received no letter from you by this ship [the *Fortune,* which arrived at Cape Cod, the 9th of November 1621] ... Yet, for as much as I know you expect the performance of my promise—which was to write unto you truly and faithfully of all things—I have, therefore, at this time sent [this letter] unto you accordingly.

Referring you for further satisfaction to our more large relations [in the attached report], you shall understand that in this little time that a few of us have been here [in America], we have built seven dwelling houses [for our families]; and four for the use of the Plantation [of Plymouth Colony]; and have made preparation for diverse others.

We set [and planted upon our land during] the last spring [of 1621] some twenty acres of Indian corn and sowed some six acres of barley and peas. And according to the manner of the Indians, we manured [or fertilized] our ground with herrings, or rather shads, which we have in great abundance and take with great ease at our doors *[from fishing in Town Brook, upon which sits Plymouth]*.

Our corn did prove well. And God be praised, we had a good increase of Indian corn, and our barley [was] indifferent—[moderately] good. But our peas [were] not worth the gathering, for we feared they were too late sown. (They came up very well and blossomed, but the sun parched them in the blossom.)

[First Thanksgiving, Autumn 1621][1]

Our harvest being gotten in, our governor [William Bradford][2] sent four men *on-fowling [bird hunting]* that so we might, after a more special manner, rejoice together after we had gathered the fruit of our labors. They four [hunters] in one day killed as much fowl [as many more men in England] as with a little help beside[s]. [Their hunt] served the company [of our people] almost a week, at which time amongst other recreations, we exercised our arms—[practiced shooting and marching].

Wild Turkey

Many of the Indians [joined our celebration]. [Some were from far away], coming amongst us and amongst the rest [of the local tribes]. Their greatest king [was] *Massasoit*, with some ninety men, whom for three days we entertained and feasted [with food from our harvest and hunt].

And they [the Indians] went out and killed five deer, which they brought to the plantation and bestowed on our governor and upon the captain [Miles Standish, leader of the militia] and others. And although it be not always so plentiful as it was at this time with us ... yet, by the goodness of God, we are so far from want that we often wish you partakers of our plenty.

White-Tailed Deer

We have found the Indians very faithful in their covenant of peace with us—very loving and ready to pleasure us. We often go to them, and they come to us. Some of us have been fifty miles by land in the country with them.

---

1   The exact date is unknown, but it was before November 9, 1621.
2   John Carver, the first governor, suffered a stroke and died in April of 1621. The Pilgrims elected William Bradford, a co-author of this book, in his place.

[Concerning] the occasions [of meeting Indians] and relations whereof, you shall understand [our success in establishing peace] by [reading] our general and more full declaration of such things as are worth the noting:

Yea, it hath pleased God so to possess the Indians with a fear of us—and love unto us. That not only the greatest king amongst them, called *Massasoit*, but also all the princes and peoples round about us, have either made suit unto us [by opening negotiations] or been glad of any occasion to make peace with us, so that seven of them at once have sent their messengers to us to that end.

Yea, [distant Indians from] an isle at sea *[Capawack, present-day Martha's Vineyard, Massachusetts]* which we never saw, hath also, together with the former [tribes of local Indians], yielded willingly to be under the protection and subjects to our sovereign, Lord King James.

[The result is] so that there is now great peace amongst the Indians themselves, which was not formerly—[and] neither would have been but for us. And we, for our parts, walk as peaceably and safely in the wood[s] as in the highways in England. We entertain them [the Indians] familiarly in our houses, and they [are] as friendly, bestowing their venison on us.

They are a people without any religion or knowledge of any god —yet [are] very trusty, quick of apprehension, ripe-witted, just. The men and women go naked, only a skin about their middles.

[A Contented Land]

For the temper of the air here, it agreeth well with that in England, and if there be any difference at all, this is somewhat hotter in summer. Some think it to be colder in winter, but I cannot out of experience so say. The air is very clear—and not foggy as hath been reported. I never in my life remember a more seasonable year than we have here enjoyed. And if we have once but *kine [cattle]*, horses, and sheep, I make no question, but men might live as contented here as in any part of the world.

For fish and fowl, we have great abundance. Fresh cod in the summer is, but course, meat with us. Our bay is full of lobsters all the summer and affordeth variety of other fish.

In September, we can take a hogshead [or barrel] of eels in a night with small labor and can dig them out of their [creek] beds. All the winter, we have mussels (and of thus)[1] at our doors. Oysters we have none near, but we can have them brought by the Indians when we will—[whenever we ask for them].

All the springtime, the earth sendeth forth naturally very good salad herbs. Here are grapes, white and red, and very sweet and strong; also strawberries, gooseberries, *raspas [raspberry]*, etc.; plums of three sorts, with black and red being almost as good as a *damson [a European plum]*; abundance of roses, white, red, and damask—single [ray of petals], but very sweet indeed.

The country wanteth only industrious men to employ. For it would grieve your hearts if, as I, you had seen so many miles together by goodly rivers uninhabited—and withal, to consider those parts of the world wherein you live to be even greatly burthened with abundance of people.

These things I thought good to let you understand, being the truth of things as near as I could experimentally take knowledge of, and [hoping] that you might on [our] behalf give God thanks— Who hath dealt so favorably with us.

[Alarm & Joy]

[New people arrived.] Our supply of men from you came the 9th of November 1621 [on the ship *Fortune*], putting in at Cape Cod, some eight or ten leagues *[twenty-four to thirty miles]* from us. The

---

1 *Of thus* refers to things similar to mussels. The 1622 text is *Othus,* a misprint. Other interpretations could be *clams, cockles,* or *other shellfish.*

Indians that dwell thereabout were they who were owners of the corn which we found in caves [and] for which we have given them full content [in repayment].

And [we] are in great league [of friendship] with them. They sent us word there was a ship near unto them but thought it to be a Frenchman [come to attack].[1] And indeed, for ourselves we expected not a friend so soon. But when we perceived that she made for our bay, the governor commanded a great [cannon] piece to be shot off to call home such as were abroad at work.

Whereupon every man—yea, boy—that could handle a gun were ready with full resolution: that if she [the strange ship] were an enemy, we would stand in our just defense, not fearing them. But God provided better for us than we supposed.

These [new people] came all in health unto us, not any being sick by the way—otherwise than by sea-sickness—and so continue [in good health] at this time by the blessing of God. (The good-wife [Martha] Ford was delivered of a son the first night she landed, and both of them are very well.)

When it pleaseth God [and] we are settled and fitted for the fishing business and other trading, I doubt not but by the blessing of God [that] the gain will give content to all.

In the meantime, [all the furs and wood] that we have gotten, we have sent by this ship. And though it be not much, yet it will witness for us that we have not been idle, considering the smallness of our number [of people] all this summer.[2]

We hope the merchants will accept of it [that they will look favorably upon the goods we have shipped] and be encouraged to furnish us with things needful for further employment, which will also encourage us to put forth ourselves to the uttermost.

---

1 French ships often plundered English colonies and ships, and vice versa.
2 Only 52 of the original 102 Pilgrims survived the first winter of 1620-1621.

[Necessary Supplies]

Now, because I expect your coming unto us with other of our friends—whose company we much desire—I thought good to advertise you of a few things needful:

Be careful to have a very good bread-room [aboard your ship] to put your biscuits in. Let your cask for beer and water be iron-bound for *the first tire—[the first hoop-fastener of your wood casks]*—if not more.[1] Let not your meat be dry-salted [before boarding ship]; none can better do it than the sailors.

Let your [flour] meal be so hard-trod in your cask, that you shall need an *adze [a small ax]* or hatchet to work it out with. Trust not too much on us for corn at this time, for by reason of this last company [of  people from the ship *Fortune*] that came depending wholly upon us, we shall have little enough till harvest. Be careful to come by some of your [flour] meal to spend [for eating] by the way [during the voyage to America]; it will much refresh you.

 Build your cabins as open as you can, and bring good store of clothes and bedding with you. Bring every man a musket or fowling [gun]-piece; let your piece be long in the barrel, and fear not the weight of it. For most of our shooting is from stands [of thick reeds, waiting for birds to pass].[2]

Bring juice of lemons and take it fasting—[sip it on an empty stomach]; it is of good use [for health].[3] [To add flavor] for hot waters, *aniseed water [licorice extract]* is the best, but use it sparingly. If you bring anything for comfort in the country, butter or salad oil, or both, is very good.

Our Indian corn—even the coarsest—maketh as pleasant meat [or staple food] as rice. There-

---

1 Water casks or barrels were made of wood slats, bound with metal hoops.
2 *Stands* could also be forked rods (above) to support heavy guns for better aim.
3 The Pilgrims seem to know that lemons cure scurvy. They may have learned this from the Dutch; the English navy did not discover lemon's benefits until 1753. Vitamin C, the curative agent in lemons, was not isolated until 1932.

fore, spare that [purchase of rice] unless to spend by the way [for your meals aboard ship during the voyage to America].

Bring paper and linseed oil for your windows[1] [of houses here], with [wicks of] cotton yarn for your lamp. Let your *shot [bullets or lead pellets for firing from guns]*[2] be [of the kind used] most for big fowls, and bring [ample] store of [gun]powder and *shot*.

I forbear further to write for the present, hoping to see you by the next return [of a ship to visit us]. So I take my leave, commending you to the LORD for a safe conduct unto us.

Resting in Him,

    Plymouth in New England
    this 11th of December 1621.[3]

                      Your loving friend
                            E. W.
                        [Edward Winslow]

---

1. Oiled paper was used for windows in lieu of glass, which was then very expensive.
2. Post-medieval *shot* could be either ball-shaped bullets or akin to modern shotgun pellets, e.g., *buckshot*. See the reference to *hail-shot* on page 104.
3. Two days later, on December 13, 1621, the ship *Fortune* sailed for England, carrying this report home for publication the following year. However, the *Fortune* was intercepted by a French warship and plundered, echoing Edward Winslow's fears. Miraculously, this report and its caretaker, Robert Cushman, survived the ordeal, reaching England on February 14, 1622.

[Appendix B – Reasons for America]

[Editor's Note: Some people in England, including fellow religious reformers, criticized the Pilgrims for abandoning England for America. The critics complained that the Pilgrims had no mandate from God to settle a new world.

Robert Cushman, a church deacon of the Pilgrims, responded with the below theological treatise; he refers to biblical passages in the margins.[1] Although he had only a limited knowledge of America, Mr. Cushman well articulates the religious sincerity of the Pilgrims and their faith in rational analysis as a means to determine God's will.]

> Reasons & considerations touching
> the lawfulness of removing out of
> England into the parts of America.

Forasmuch as many exceptions are daily made against the going into and inhabiting of foreign desert[ed] places—[and critics seek] to the hindrances of plantations abroad and the increase of distractions at home [here in England]—it is not amiss that some which have been earwitnesses of the exceptions made (and are either agents or abettors of such removals and plantation) do seek to give *content [satisfactory reply]* to the world in all things that possibly they can. `The Preamble`

And [those going abroad are honorable], although the most of the opposites—[those critics staying here in England]—are such as either dream of raising their fortunes here—to that [selfish purpose] then, which there is nothing more unlike [the people going overseas]; or [the critics are] such as affecting their home-born country [England] so vehemently, as that they had rather with all their friends beg, yea, starve in it than[2] undergo a little difficulty in seeking [new lands] abroad.

[Sincere People] — Yet, are there some who, out of doubt [and] in tenderness of conscience, [are truly sincere] and fear to offend God by running [to America] before they be called [by Him to go there]? Are [these people] *straitened [restricted],* and do [they] straiten others from going to foreign plantations?

---

1 Margin notes are abbreviated, e.g., "*Reas.*" for reason. Updated biblical abbreviations include "*Matt.*" for Matthew; "*Ps.*" for Psalms; "*Gen.*" for Genesis; etc.
2 The 1622 text often uses *then* for *than*. This edition corrects such instances.

[It is to these sincere people] for whose cause especially I have been drawn. Out of my good affection to them, [I seek] to publish some reasons that might give them content and satisfaction—and also stay and stop the willful and witty caviler. And herein, I trust I shall not be blamed of any *godly-wise [arrogance]*, though through my slender judgment, I should miss the mark and not strike the nail on the head. Considering it is the first attempt that hath been made (that I know of) to defend those enterprises [in America], reason would therefore [require] that if any man of deeper reach and better judgment see further or otherwise [have a better answer], that he rather instruct me than deride me.

[Word of God] — And being studious for brevity, we must first consider that whereas God of old did call and summon our fathers—by predictions, dreams, visions, and certain illuminations—to go from their countries, places, and habitations to reside and dwell here or there; and to wander up and down from city to city, and land to land, according to His will and pleasure ... Now there is no such calling to be expected for any matter whatsoever.

| Cautions. Gen. 12: 1, 2. & 35: 1. |

Matt. 2: 19.
Ps. 105: 13.

Heb. 1: 1, 2.

Neither must any[one] so much as imagine that there will now be any such thing. God did once so train up his people [to go to new lands directly upon hearing His voice], but now he doth not. But [God] speaks in another manner, and so we must apply ourselves to God's present dealing—and not to his wonted dealing [in historical times].

Josh. 5: 12.

And as the miracle of giving *manna [food from Heaven]* ceased when the fruits of the land became plenty, so God [ceases to directly order us to go to new lands], having such a plentiful storehouse of [previous] directions in His holy word. There must not now [be] any extraordinary [new] revelations [to] be expected.

But now [we must study God's previous directions]—the ordinary examples and precepts of the scriptures reasonably and rightly understood and applied. [They] must be the voice and word [of God] that must call us, press us, and direct us in every action.

[Holy Land] — Neither is there any land or possession now like unto the possession which the Jews had in Canaan, being legally holy and appropriated [by God] unto a holy people, *the seed Abraham—[the heirs of the prophet Abraham, the Father of the Hebrews]*—in which they dwelt securely and had their days pro-

Gen. 17: 8.

longed. [Only the Hebrews received such land], it being by an immediate voice [that] said that He (the Lord) gave it [to] them as a land of rest after their weary travels and [as] a type of eternal rest in Heaven. But now there is no land of that sanctimony, no land so appropriated, none typical, much less any that can be said to be given of God to any nation as was Canaan—which they and their seed must dwell in till God sendeth upon them sword or captivity.

But now we are, in all places, strangers and pilgrims, travelers and sojourners—most properly having no dwelling but in this earthen tabernacle. Our dwelling [in this life] is but a wandering; and our abiding [on earth], but as a fleeting [moment in time].

| 2 Cor. 5: 1,2,3. |

And in a word, our home is nowhere but in the heavens, in that house not made with hands [but] whose maker and builder is God, and to which all ascend that love the coming of our Lord Jesus.

| So were the Jews, but yet their temporal blessings and inheritances were more large than ours. |

Though then, there may be reasons to persuade a man to live in this or that land—yet, there cannot be the same reasons which the Jews had. But now as natural civil and religious bands tie men [together in society], so they must be bound [even when new lands appear]. And as good reasons [to move] for things *terrene [earthly]* and heavenly appear, so they [the people] must be led [to new lands].

[*Life's Meaning*] — And so here falleth in our question, how a man that is here [in England] borne and bred, and hath lived some years, may remove himself into another country.

| *Objection.* |

I answer: A man must not respect only to live and do good to himself, but he should see where he can live to do most good to others. For as one saith, *He whose living is but for himself—it is time he were dead.* [Original italics.]

| *Answer.* 1 What persons may hence remove [to America]. |

Some men there are who, of necessity, must here [in England] live as being tied to duties [and being obligated] either to Church, commonwealth, household, kindred, etc. But others —and that [are] many—[are those] who do no good in none of those, nor can do none [because they are] as being not able or not in favor [of doing such duties]. Or [they are] as wanting opportunity and live as outcasts, nobodies, eyesores—eating but for themselves; teaching but themselves; and doing good to none, either in soul or body—and so pass over days, years, and months—yea, so live and so die.

Now such [hopeless people in England] should lift up their eyes and see whether there be not some other place and country to which they may go to do good. And [they may yet] have use towards [benefiting] others of that knowledge, wisdom, humanity, reason, strength, skill, faculty, etc., which God hath given them for the service of others and His own glory.

| 2 Why they should remove [to America]. |

But [I want] not to pass the bounds of modesty, so far as to name any [who should go abroad]—though I confess I know many who sit here still with their talent in a napkin, having notable endowments, both of body and mind, and might do great good if they were in some places [in distant lands]. [But they] which [are] here do [good for] none nor can do none—and yet, through fleshly fear, *niceness [weakness], straitness of heart [timidity]*, etc., sit still and look on [while others go to America]. And [they] will not hazard a dram of health nor a day of pleasure nor an hour of rest to further the knowledge and salvation of *the sons of Adam—[the heirs of the first man created by God]*—in that New World where a drop of the knowledge of Christ is most precious [but] which is here [in England] not set-by [or respected]. Now what shall we say to such a procession of Christ [going to America] to which is joined no more denial of a man's self [his basic need to do good]?

| *Luke 19: 20.* |

| Reas. 1. |

[Heathen's Country] — But some will say, "What right have I to go live in the heathen's country [that which belongs to the native Indians]?"

| Objection. |

[I answer first by] letting pass the ancient discoveries, contracts, and agreements which our Englishmen have long since made in those parts, together with the acknowledgment of the histories and chronicles of other nations who profess [that] the land of America from the Cape *de* Florida unto the *Bay of Canado [Hudson Bay in Canada]*—which is South and North 300 leagues *[900 miles]* and upwards; and [between] East and West [is] further than yet hath been discovered —is proper to the King of England.

| Answer. |

Yet, letting that pass—lest I be thought to meddle further than it concerns me, or further than I have discerning—I will mention such things as are within my reach [of] knowledge, sight, and practice, since I have travailed in these affairs.

And first, seeing we daily pray for the conversion of the
heathens, we must consider whether there be not some ordinary means and course for us to take to convert them, or whether prayer for them be only referred to God's extraordinary work from heaven.

Reas. 2.

Now it seemeth unto me that we ought also to endeavor and use the [ordinary] means to convert them—and the means cannot be used unless we go to them or they come to us. To us, they cannot come; our land is full. To them, we may go; their land is empty.

Reas. 3.

This then is a sufficient reason to prove our going thither to live [is] lawful. Their land is spacious and void, and there are few [people], and [they] do but run over the grass, as do also the foxes and wild beasts. They [the native people] are not industrious; neither [do they] have art, science, skill, or faculty to use either the land or the commodities of it—but all spoils, rots, and is marred for want of manuring, gathering, ordering, etc.

[Editor's Note: Robert Cushman was incorrect about Indian agriculture; it was highly productive. The Pilgrims discovered that the Native Americans were clearing and planting huge tracts of land for crops. The Indians later taught the Pilgrims many of their agricultural skills.]

As the ancient patriarchs therefore removed from straiter places [migrating from lands crowded with too many people] into more roomthy *[sic]* where the land lay idle and waste, and none used it, though there dwelt inhabitants by them—as [written in the passages of the Bible] *Genesis 13: 6, 11, 12;* and *34: 21;* and *41: 20*—so is it lawful now to take a land which none useth and make use of it.

Reas. 4.
This is to be considered as respecting New England, and the territories about the plantation.

[Consent of the Indians] — And as it is a common land, or unused and undressed country, so we have [obtained] it by common consent, composition, and agreement—[and] which agreement is double [in meaning]:

First, the Imperial Governor *Massasoit*—[the Indian ruler] whose circuits [of territory] in likelihood are larger than England and Scotland—hath acknowledged the King's Majesty of England to be his master and commander. And that once in my hearing [and presence][1]—yea, and in writing under his hand to Captain Standish [military advisor at Plymouth]—both he *[Massasoit]* and many other kings which are under him as [Indian governors of] *Pamet [River], Nauset, Cummaquid, Narrowhiggonset [Narragansett], Nemasket, etc.*, with diverse others that

---

1   Robert Cushman visited the Pilgrims in 1621. See page 13.

dwell about the bays of *Patuxet [Plymouth]* and *Massachusetts [Boston Bay]* [have submitted to the King of England].

Neither hath this been accomplished by threats and blows, or shaking of sword and sound of trumpet, for as our faculty that way is small, and our strength less. So our warring with them is after another manner, namely by *friendly usage [good diplomatic relations]*—love, peace, honest and just carriages, good counsel, etc.

That [being] so, we and they may not only live in peace in that land, and they [the Indians] yield subjection to an earthly prince, but that as voluntaries, they may be persuaded at length to embrace the Prince of Peace, Christ Jesus, and rest in peace with Him forever. *Ps. 110: 3. & 48: 3.*

Secondly, this composition [with the Indians] is also more particular and applicatory as touching [only] ourselves there inhabiting. The emperor [of the Indians], by a joint consent, hath promised and appointed us to live at peace where we will in all his dominions—taking what place we will; and as much land as we will; and bringing as many people as we will—and that [all of this is granted] for these two causes:

- First, because we are the servants of James, King of England, whose [title to] the land, as he [the Indian emperor] confesseth, is [proper];
- Secondly, because he [the Indian emperor] hath found us just, honest, kind, and peaceable—and so loves our company. Yea, and that in these things, there is no dissimulation on his part nor fear of breach—except our [need for] security [may yet] engender in them some unthought-of treachery, or our uncivility provoke them to anger.

[The friendship of the Indians] is most plain in other relations which show that the things they did were more out of love than out of fear.

[The Land is Freely Given] — [Hence, our move to America is proper because:]

- First, [the land] being then first a vast and empty chaos;
- Secondly, [the native people] acknowledged the right of our sovereign King [of England];
- Thirdly, by a peaceable composition, [an agreement] in part possessed of diverse of his loving subjects [the Indians themselves].

[Therefore], I see not who can doubt or call in question the lawfulness of inhabiting or dwelling there [in America]. But [rather, I believe] that it may be as lawful (for such as are not tied upon some special occasion here [in England]) to live there, as well as here.

Yea, and as the enterprise is weighty and difficult, so the honor is more worthy to plant a rude wilderness—to enlarge the honor and fame of our dread sovereign [King James of England]. But chiefly [we seek] to display the efficacy and power of the Gospel, both *[sic]* in zealous preaching, professing, and wise-walking under it before the faces of these poor, blind infidels.

[Fear is No Excuse] — As for such [people] as object [to] the tediousness of the voyage thither [to America], the danger of pirates' robbery, of the savages' treachery, etc.—these are but lions in the way.

> Prov. 22: 13.

And it were well for such men, if they were [already] in heaven. For who can show them a place in this world where iniquity shall not compass them at the heels, and where they shall have a day without grief—or a lease of life for a moment [longer than God intends]?

> Ps. 49: 5.
> Matt. 6: 34.

And who can tell but God what dangers may lie at our doors, even in our native country, or what plots may be abroad, or when God will cause our sun to go down at noondays and, in the midst of our peace and security, lay upon us some lasting scourge for our so long neglect and contempt of His most glorious Gospel?

> Amos 8: 9.

> Objection.

[Forsake Comfort?] — But we have here [in England] great peace, plenty of the Gospel, and many sweet delights and variety of comforts.

> Answer.
> 2 Chro. 32: 25.

True, indeed—and far be it from us to deny and diminish the least of these mercies—but have we rendered unto God thankful obedience for this long peace whilst other peoples have been at war? Have we not hither murmured, repined, and fallen *at jars [in conflict]* amongst ourselves whilst our peace hath lasted with foreign power[s]? Was there ever more suits in law, more ennui, contempt, and reproach than nowadays [here in England]?

> Gen. 13: 9, 10.

Abraham and *Lot [two founders of the Hebrews]* departed asunder when there fell a breach betwixt them, which was occasioned by *the straitness [the difficulty]* of the land. And surely I am persuaded that howsoever, the frailties of men are principal in all contentions.

Yet, the straitness of the place [here in England] is such as each man is *fain [inclined]* to pluck his means [for a livelihood], as it were, out of his neighbor's throat. There is such pressing and oppressing in town and country about farms, trades, traffic, etc., so as a man can hardly anywhere set up *a trade [a small business]*, but he shall [also] pull down two of his neighbors.

The towns abound with young tradesmen [who are unemployed], and the hospitals are full of the ancient [elderly people]. The country is replenished with [too many] new farmers, and the almshouses are filled with old laborers. Many there are who get their living with bearing burdens, but more are fain to burden the land with their whole bodies. Multitudes get their means of life by *prating [idle chatter]*,[1] and so do numbers more by begging.

Neither come these straits upon men always through *intemperancy [drunkenness], ill husbandry [waste]*, indiscretion, etc., as some think. But even the most wise, sober, and discreet men go often to the wall when they have done their best.

Wherein, as God's providence swayeth all, so it is easy to see that the straitness of the place [in England], having in it so many strait hearts [or so many cruel men], cannot but produce such effects more and more.

So, as every indifferent [or fair]-minded man should be ready to say with Father Abraham, *"Take then, the right hand, and I will take the left,"* **[original italics]** let us not thus oppress, straiten, and afflict one another. But [rather], seeing there is a spacious land [in America]—the way to which is through the sea—we will end this difference [and conflict] in a day.

[Religious Disputes] — [Regarding our greatest conflict], that I speak nothing about the bitter contention that hath been about religion. [We waste effort] by writing, disputing, and inveighing earnestly one against another, the heat of which zeal, if it were turned against the rude barbarism of the heathens, it might do more good in a day than it hath done here [in England] in many years.

[In America, we shall have] neither of the little love [shown] to the Gospel and [nor] profit which is made by the preachers in most places. [We leave behind such corruption] which might easily drive the zealous to the heathens—who, no doubt, if they had but a drop of that [religious] knowledge which here flieth about the streets, would be filled with exceeding great joy and gladness. [Many in England are not

---

1 *Prating* may be beggars giving long-winded speeches to entertain passersby, who contribute coins. Or it could be a misprint for *pirating*, i.e., *plunder*.

as virtuous] as that; they would even pluck the Kingdom of Heaven by violence and take it, as it were, by force.

[Friends Separate] — The greatest *let [obstacle]* that is yet [to be left] behind is the sweet fellow[ship] of friends and the satiety of bodily delights [here in England]. But can there be two nearer friends almost than *Abraham [father of the Hebrews]* and *Lot [Abraham's nephew]*? Or than *Paul and Barnabas [early Christian missionaries]*?

> The last *let* [or obstacle to reaching America].

And yet upon as little occasions as we have here, they departed asunder—two of them being patriarchs of the Church of Old; [and] the other[s], the Apostles of the [Christian] Church, which is new. And their covenants were such as it seemeth might bind as much as any covenant between men at this day. And yet to avoid greater inconveniences, they departed asunder.

[Pleasures are Fleeting] — Neither must men take so much thought for the [pleasures of the] flesh as not to be pleased except [that] they can pamper their bodies with [a] variety of dainties. Nature is content with little, and health is much endangered by [exotic] mixtures upon the stomach. The delights of the palate do often inflame the vital parts, as the tongue setteth a fire [to] the whole body.

> James 3: 6.

Secondly, varieties [of food] here [in England] are not common to all, but many good men are glad to snap at a crust. The rent-taker lives on sweet morsels, but the rent-payer eats a dry crust—often with watery eyes.

And it is nothing to say what [luxury] some one of a hundreth hath, but [it is important] what the bulk, body, and commonalty [of most people] hath, which, I warrant you, is short enough. And they also which now live so sweetly [may soon suffer]. Hardly will their children attain to that privilege, but some *circumventor [a trickster]* or other will outstrip them—and make them sit in the dust, to which men are brought in one age but cannot get out of it again in seven generations.

[The Godly to America] — To conclude, without all partiality, *the present consumption [the current suffering]* which groweth upon us here [in England], whilst the land groaneth under so many closefisted and unmerciful men—being compared with the easiness, plainness, and plentifulness in living in those remote places [of America]—may quickly persuade any man to a liking of this course and to practice a removal

[to a far-away land], which being done by honest, godly, and industrious men, they shall there be right-heartily welcome.

But for other [men] of dissolute and profane life, *their rooms are better than their company's—[their opportunity for misdeeds will be greater than for those who remain behind].* For if here [in England], where the Gospel hath been so long and plentifully taught, they are yet frequent in such vices as the heathen would shame to speak of, what will they be [in a far-away land] when there is less restraint in word and deed?

My only *suit [request]* to all men is that whether they live there or here, they would learn to use this world as they used it not—keeping faith and a good conscience, both with God and men—[such] that when the day of account [before God] shall come, they may come forth as good and fruitful servants, and freely be received and enter into the joy of their Master.

      R. C.
      [Robert Cushman][1]

---

1 Robert Cushman was a business agent and lay official of the Pilgrim church. He visited the Pilgrims in America in 1621. See page 13.

[Appendix C – The First Preface]

To His Much Respected
Friend, Mr. J. P.[1]

Good Friend: As we cannot but account [that] it [is] an extraordinary blessing of God in directing our course for these parts [of America] after we came out of our native country—[and] for that [reason], we had the happiness to be possessed of the comforts we receive by the benefit of one of the most pleasant, most healthful, and most fruitful parts of the world—so [therefore] must we acknowledge the same blessing to be multiplied upon our whole company [of like-minded people].

For that [purpose], we obtained the honor to receive allowance and approbation of our free possession [of land in America]. And enjoying [that grant] thereof under the authority of those thrice-honored persons,[2] the President and Council for the affairs of New England, by whose bounty and grace in that behalf [we receive the land], all of us are tied to dedicate our best service unto them as those under His Majesty [King James of England] that we owe it unto. [We serve those] whose noble endeavors in these, their actions [in colonizing New England], the God of heaven and earth multiply to His glory and their own eternal comforts.

As for *this poor relation [this humble report],* I pray you to accept it as being writ by the several actors themselves, after their plain and rude manner. Therefore, doubt nothing of the truth thereof. If it be defective in anything, it is their ignorance [of grammar]; [they are people] that are better acquainted with planting than writing. If it satisfy those that are well affected to the business [of establishing a new colony in America], it is all I care for.

---

1   *J.P.* was John Pierce, an agent of the Pilgrims in London.
2   "Thrice-honored" probably refers to several, successive grants of legal authority by the English King to the Council for New England for establishing colonies in America. The Council was one of two "Virginia" companies; both granted land to the Pilgrims.

Sure I am [that] the place we are in—and the hopes that are apparent—cannot but suffice any [person] that will not desire more than enough [for his needs]. Neither is there want of ought among us [in America] but company to enjoy the blessings so plentifully bestowed upon the inhabitants that are here.

While I was a writing this, I had almost forgot that I had but [offer] the recommendation of the relation itself—[I need only present to you the following report] to your further consideration. And therefore, I will end without saying more, save that I shall always rest

> From Plymouth in
> New England.
>
> > Yours in the way of friendship,
> > *R. G. [R.C.]* [1]
> > *[Robert Cushman]*

---

1 *R.G.* is an alias or misprint from 1622. *R.C.* or Robert Cushman was an agent of the Pilgrims in London. He visited the Pilgrims in America in the autumn of 1621 and carried this report back to England. See page 13.

[Appendix D – The Second Preface]

[Editor's Note: The Second Preface is by a mysterious "G. Mourt," the only contributor to provide his surname rather than merely his initials. He is the basis of the original nickname for this report, *Mourt's Relation*.

However, the identity of "G. Mourt" has never been firmly established. Some think he was George Morton, a business agent of the Pilgrims in England. Mr. Morton helped publish *Mourt's Relation* and later emigrated to America to join the Pilgrims. However, he neither claimed authorship of any part of the report nor displayed other literary talents.

"G. Mourt" may only be a phantom, a coy concoction by the Pilgrims to evade censorship by a hostile English government. *Mort* is Latin for death; *mort's relation* would be a malapropism, i.e., a report from the dead. Indeed, the whimsical tone of this preface suggests a sly pun, needling critics who predicted the Pilgrims would perish in the wilderness of America.]

* * * *

To the Reader:

Courteous Reader: Be entreated to make a favorable construction of my forwardness in publishing these ensuing discourses. [My friends hath] the desire of carrying the Gospel of Christ into those foreign parts [and] amongst those people that as yet have had no knowledge nor taste of God; [and] as also to procure unto themselves and others a quiet and comfortable habitation.

[These reasons] were, amongst other things, the inducements unto these undertakers of the then hopeful (and now experimentally known) good enterprise for plantation in New England. [My friends sought] to set afoot and prosecute the same, and though it fared [well] with them, [it is also true], as it is common to the most actions of this nature, that the first attempts prove difficult, as the sequel [in the following pages] more at large expresseth.

Yet, it hath pleased God, eve[n] beyond our expectation in so short a time, to give hope of letting some of them see (though some He hath taken out of this vale of tears) some grounds of hope of the accomplishment of both those end[s] by them as first propounded.[1]

---

1 The 1622 text is "*at* first propounded," a probable misprint.

And as myself then much desired and shortly hope to effect [a journey to America]—if the Lord will [permit] the putting to, of my shoulder in this hopeful business—[I wanted to learn more about those foreign places]. And in the meantime, these relations [these following reports about America] coming to my hand from my both known and faithful friends on whose writings I do much rely, I thought it not amiss to make them more general [in circulation], hoping of a cheerful proceeding, both of *adventurers [investors]* and *planters [colonists]*.

[And I close by] entreating that the example of the honorable Virginia and Bermudas Companies—encountering with so many disasters [in their American colonies] and [enduring] that for diverse years together with an unwearied resolution (the good effects whereof are now eminent)—may prevail as a spur of preparation [for other companies to establish more colonies].

Also, touching this no less hopeful country [of America], though yet an infant—the extent and commodities whereof are as yet not fully known—after time [her true nature] will unfold more. Such [people] as desire to take knowledge of [these] things may inform themselves by this ensuing treatise and, if they please, also by [speaking to] such as have been there a first and second time.

My hearty prayer to God is that the event of this [colony of New Plymouth in America], and all other honorable and honest undertakings, may be for the furtherance of the Kingdom of Christ; the enlarging of the bounds of our Sovereign Lord, King James; and the good and profit of those who, either by purse or person, or both, are agents in the same.

So I take leave and rest,

Thy friend,
G. MOURT[1]

---

1 Either a pseudonym for George Morton, a business agent of the Pilgrims, or a sly pun. See previous Editor's Note.

[Appendix E – The Third Preface]

[Editor's Note: The Third Preface was a reprint of a sermon by the minister of the Pilgrims, John Robinson. He wrote the sermon for passengers of the *Mayflower* as they prepared for departure to America in 1620. The Pilgrims later credited the sermon as a guiding light for their endeavors.

John Robinson, however, remained behind in Holland, the former refuge for the exiled Pilgrims. He planned to sail on a later ship after helping others emigrate to America. John Robinson, however, died in 1625 at age 50 while still in Holland. Sadly, he never reached America.]

* * * *

CERTAIN USEFUL
ADVERTISEMENTS *[or Advice]* SENT
in a Letter written by a discreet friend
unto the Planters in New England at their first setting
sail from Southampton [England], [and] who earnestly desireth
the prosperity of that, their new
Plantation.

Loving and Christian friends: I do heartily and in the Lord salute you all, as being they with whom I am present—[your friends and family here in Holland also send their greetings].[1] [I keep you] in my best affection and most earnest longings after you, though I be constrained for a while to be bodily absent from you. I say constrained [because] God knowing how willingly and much rather than otherwise I would have borne my part[2] with you in this first brunt [of the long voyage to America], were I not, by strong necessity, held back for the present. Make [kindly] account of me in the meanwhile as of a man divided in myself with great pain and—as natural bonds set aside—having my better part with you.

---

1 Only 102 passengers sailed aboard the *Mayflower*. Several hundred would-be Pilgrims remained behind in Holland, their home-in-exile. They planned to sail later, depending on the outcome of the *Mayflower's* voyage.

2 The 1622 text has a duplicate word: "I would have *have* borne my part..."

And though I doubt not but in your godly wisdoms—you both foresee and resolve [wisely] upon that which concerneth your present state and condition, both severally and jointly—yet have I thought but my duty [is] to add some further spur of provocation unto them who run already, if not because you need it [but rather] yet because I owe it in love and duty.

[Acknowledge Faults]

And first, as we are daily to renew our repentance with our God—especially[1] for our sins known and general[ly] for our unknown trespasses—so doth the Lord call us in a singular manner (upon occasions of such difficulty and danger as lieth upon you) to a both more narrow search and careful reformation of our ways in His fight. [We do these things] lest, He, [when] calling to remembrance our sins—[those] forgotten by us or unrepented of—take advantage against us and, in judgment, [condemn and] leave us for the same, to be swallowed up in one danger or other.

Whereas, on the contrary, [if] sin being taken away by earnest repentance and the pardon thereof from the Lord—sealed up unto a man's conscience by His Spirit—great shall be his security and peace in all dangers; sweet, his comforts in all distresses; with happy deliverance from all evil, whether in life or in death.

[Forgive Others]

Now next, after this heavenly peace with God and our own confidences [that acknowledge our sins], we are carefully to provide for peace with all men—[knowing] what [faults] in us lieth—especially with our associates. And for that end, watchfulness must be had that we neither at all in ourselves do give—no, nor easily take—offense being given by others.

Woe be unto the world for offenses. For though it be necessary (considering the malice of Satan and man's corruption) that offenses come, yet woe unto the man or woman either by whom the offense cometh, saith Christ (*Matthew 18: 7*).[2]

---

1 The 1622 text is "*special* for our sins," and probably incorrect. See footnote (g) of *Mourt's Relation* (Boston: John Kimball Wiggon, 1865), p. xlii.
2 These are biblical references from the original text of 1622.

And if offenses in the *unseasonable [improper]* use of things [that are] in themselves indifferent be more to be feared than death itself—as the Apostle teacheth *(1 Corinthian 9: 15)*—how much more [is there to fear] in things simply evil, in which neither honor of God nor love of man is thought worthy to be regarded?

Neither yet is it sufficient that we keep ourselves, by the grace of God, from giving offense, except withal we be armed against the taking of them when they are given by others. For how imperfect and lame is the work of Grace in that person who wants *charity [forgiveness]* to cover a multitude of [his] offenses, as the Scriptures speak?

[Frailty & Strangers]

[I urge you to follow the true Grace of God.] Neither are you to be exhorted to this Grace only upon the common grounds of Christianity. [Beware of missteps], which are that persons ready to take offense either want charity to cover [their] offenses, or wisdom duly to weigh [their] human frailty; or lastly [they] are gross, though *close [secret]* hypocrites, as Christ our Lord teacheth *(Matthew 7: 1, 2, 3).*

As indeed in mine own experience, few or none have been found which sooner give offense than such as easily take it. Neither have they ever proved sound and profitable members in societies which have nourished in themselves that touchy humor.

But besides these [matters], here are diverse special motives provoking you above others to great care and conscience [in dealing with new people] this way: As first, you are, many of you, strangers as to the persons. So [you know not] to the infirmities [of] one of another, and so stand in need of more watchfulness this way —lest, when such things fall out in men and women as you suspected not, you [will] be inordinately affected with them (which doth require, at your hands, much wisdom and charity for the covering and preventing of incident offenses that way).

[Patience]

And lastly, your intended course of civil community [and the establishment of local government] will minister continual occasion of offense and will be as fuel for that fire [of personal conflict]—except you diligently quench it with brotherly forbearance.

And if taking of offense—causally or easily at men's doings—[is to] be so carefully to be avoided, how much more heed is to be taken that we take not offense at God Himself, which yet we certainly do so oft? (As we do murmur at His Providence in our *crosses [frustrations]* or bear impatiently such afflictions as wherewith He pleaseth to visit us.) Store we up, therefore, patience against the evil day—without which, we [might] take offense at the Lord Himself in His holy and just works.

[Do Good for All]

A fourth thing there is carefully to be provided for. To wit, that with your common employments, you join common affections [for all people]. [Be] truly bent upon the general good [of society], avoiding as a deadly plague:

- [selfishness] of your both common and special comfort;
- all retiredness of mind for [im]proper advantage; and
- all singularly affected [greed], any manner of way.

Let every man repress in himself and [in] the whole body [of society represented] in each person—as so many rebels against the common good—all private respects of men's selves not sorting with the general convenience [for the betterment of society].

And as men are careful not to have a new house shaken with any violence before it be well settled and the parts firmly knit, so be you [careful in your new home]. I beseech you, brethren, [be] much more careful that the house of God—which you are, and are to be—be not shaken with unnecessary novelties or other oppositions [to brotherly love] at the first settling [in America] thereof.

[Elect and Respect Good Leaders]

Lastly, whereas

- you are to become a body politic, using amongst yourselves civil government; and
- are not furnished with any persons of special eminence above the rest to be chosen by you into office of government,

[then] let your wisdom and godliness appear not only in choosing such persons [to be leaders] as do entirely love [all the people] and will diligently promote the common good, but also in yielding unto them all due honor and obedience in their lawful administrations.

[Be] not beholding in them [your leaders] the ordinariness of their persons, but God's ordinance for your good. Nor [shall you obey them blindly] being like unto the foolish multitude who more honor *the gay coat [the outward appearance]* than either the virtuous mind of the man or [the] glorious ordinance of the Lord.

But you know better things and that the image of the Lord's power and authority which the magistrate [or government official] beareth is honorable in [no matter] how *mean [lowly]* persons soever. And [regarding] this duty [to respect officials], you both may the more willingly and ought the more conscionably to perform [such duty] because you are—at least for the present—to have only them for your ordinary governors which yourselves shall make choice of, for that work.

Sundry other things of importance, I could put you in mind of —and of those before mentioned—in more words. But I will not so far wrong your godly minds as to think you heedless of these things. (There being also diverse among you so well able to admonish both themselves and others of what concerneth them.)

[God Shall Guide & Guard]

These few things, therefore—and the same [for the other matters]—in [these] few words, I do earnestly commend unto your care and conscience, joining therewith my daily incessant prayers unto the Lord: That He who hath made the Heavens and the earth, the sea, and all rivers of waters—and whose Providence is over all His work, especially over all His dear children for [doing] good—would so guide and guard you in your ways, as inwardly by His Spirit, so outwardly by the hand of His power.

[I so pray] as that both you and we [in Holland] also[1]—[who are] for and with you—may have [the peace of God] after [our manner][2] of praising His name, all the days of your and our lives.

Fare you well in Him, in Whom you trust, and in Whom I rest,

An unfeigned well-willer
[a genuine well-wisher]
of your happy success
in this hopeful voyage,

J.R.
[John Robinson, Minister,
Leyden, Holland, July 1620]

---

1 Most of the Pilgrim congregation, about 300 people, remained behind in Holland when the *Mayflower* sailed for America. They planned to follow later.
2 The 1622 text is "after *matter* of praising His name," a likely misprint.

Alphabetical Index

Alden, John....................................32n.
Alderton [Allerton], John................52
Allerton, Issac................68, 83, 91, 94
Allerton, Mary......................68, 83, 91
Artillery 67, 70, 82
Aspinet..110p.
Barnstable Harbor.................108, 112
Billington Sea......................74, 76, 83
Billington, Francis..........................74
Billington, John.............................108
Boston Bay.................17, 117pp., 121
Bradford, William: biography, 5; 14, 17, 33, 41, 49, 52, 75, 78, 123
Brewster, William........................79n.
Cannons (artillery)..............67, 70, 82
Cape Cod... 23, 25, 27, 31, 34, 49pp., 54, 61, 63, 67, 70, 83, 86, 97, 103, 108, 112p., 125
Cape Cod Bay........27, 37, 40, 43, 51, 55p., 57, 60p., 108
Cape Cod National Seashore.. 36, 41
Carver, John 33, 37, 42, 52, 73, 75, 78, 83, 90
Charles River................................121
Charlestown, Massachusetts.........119
Christmas Day, 1621.......................69
Clark, John....................53, 61, 64, 66
Clark's Island............................61, 66
Cold Harbor (Pamet River)............44
Cook, Francis..................................81
Coppin, Robert....................51, 60pp.
Corbitant....................................113pp.
Corn....37pp., 42, 44pp., 49, 55p., 64, 66, 72, 87, 94, 97p., 103, 105, 111p., 120, 122p., 126p.
Corn Hill.................45, 49, 55p., 90n.
Cornhill (London)....................12, 90
Courtship of Miles Standish... 32n., 82
Cummaquid 108, 112p., 133
Cushman, Robert.......13pp., 21, 129, 133, 138
Deer..37, 41, 46, 76, 80, 84, 87, 123p.

Dermer, Thomas.............................86
Dotte (or Doten), Edward.............52
East Harbor (Pilgrim Lake).......43p.
East Harbor Creek 36, 41
Eastham, Massachusetts....54pp., 59, 109pp.
English, Thomas 52
First Encounter Beach.................. 59
Ford, Martha.................................126
Fortune (ship)..............13p., 122, 125
Frenchmen....................................104
Fresh Brook Village (Wellfleet). 54n.
Fur trade (animal skins)...86, 88, 90, 97, 103pp., 110p., 120p.
Gardners Neck.............102, 105, 115
Gorges, Sir Fernando.....................86
Government........................30, 146p.
Grampus (killer whale)..............54p.
Graves...........................38, 47, 55, 97
Great Pond (Eastham, Mass.).......55
Great South Pond..........................83
Hatches Creek (See Indian Brook)
Head of the Meadow................36, 41
Hobbamock...............................113pp.
Holland....................31, 36, 143, 148
Hopkin's Creek..............................40
Hopkins, Steven.....33, 41, 52, 81, 96
Howland, John...............................52
Indian Brook (Hatches Creek).....54
Iyanough............................109p., 112
James (King of England).....30p., 90, 92, 104, 119, 124, 133p., 139, 142
Jones, Christopher........34, 42pp., 46, 59, 65, 74
Kingston, Massachusetts................65
Longfellow, Henry.................32n., 82
Maine..........................84, 85p., 119p.
Martha's Vineyard (Island)..........124
Martin, Christopher.......................73
Massachusetts....... 13, 21, 34, 65, 98, 102, 105p., 109, 111pp., 117pp., 124, 134

Massachusetts [Indians].....23, 117pp.
Massachusetts Queen......................118
Massasoit............23, 90, 92pp., 96, 98, 102pp., 111, 113p., 116, 118, 123p., 133
Mattapoiset.....................102, 105, 115
Mayflower (ship)......5, 14pp., 21, 25, 28, 30, 32pp., 40, 42p., 47, 59, 63, 65, 67pp., 72pp., 79p., 82, 86, 89, 122, 143
Mayflower Compact......................30
Mayflower Pilgrims...5, 13pp., 19, 21
Medford, Massachusetts..............120
Middleborough, Mass: ....23, 98; Titicut, 99; 106, 113
Monhegan Island.....................84, 85p.
Morton, George............21, 122, 141p.
Mourt's Relation.....11, 13, 17pp., 151
Mullins, Priscilla....................32n., 82
Mystic Lakes...............................120
Mystic River.................................121
Nemasket.........23, 98, 106, 113p., 133
Nanopashemet..............................120
Narragansett Bay.........................99
Narragansett Indians........23, 94, 101, 111, 113, 133
Narrohiggonset, Narrohiganset, or *Narrohigganset* [See *Narragansett*]
Nauset or *Nausites*. 23; fight with, 86; 108pp.; 112p.; 133
North Truro, Massachusetts... 37, 46
Obbatinewat...............................118p.
Old Tom's Hill.........................44, 51
Pamet Little River 40, 44
Paomet or Pamet River......40, 44, 49, 97, 103, 133
Patuxet................85, 89, 97, 111, 134
Penobscot River, Maine...............119
Pilgrim Heights............................36
Pilgrim Lake (See East Harbor)
Pilgrim Spring...........................37
Plymouth (America) 13p., 23, 25, 61, 63p., 66p., 72, 97, 106, 108, 111p., 114, 117, 128, 134, 140
Plymouth (England).......................25

Pokanoket........23, 86, 96, 98, 102, 107
Provincetown........27, 29, 31p., 34, 42
Quadequina ....90p.
Quincy, Massachusetts.................118
Rhode Island.......23, 96, 99, 113, 118
Robinson, John................21, 141, 148
Rock Hill....................................120
Romance of Pilgrims...............32n., 82
Samoset......................84, 87pp., 94p.
Skins (fur trade)...........86, 88, 90, 97, 103pp., 110p., 120p.
Slany, John...................................90
Sowams..................................98, 102
Squa Sachem.............................118p.
Squanto (See *Tisquantum*)
Standish, Captain Miles....33, 52, 57, 73, 81pp., 89, 91, 94, 115, 118, 133
Standish, Rose..............................83
Swansea, Mass.............102, 105, 115
Tarentines (Indians)..................119p.
Taunton (Titicut) River.........99, 106
Thanksgiving, first (1621)...........123
Thievish Harbor 51, 59
Tilley, Ann...................................83
Tilley, Edward..................33, 52, 83
Tilley, John.................................52
Tisquantum (a.k.a. Squanto) 23, 89p., 94p., 96, 98, 102, 105, 108, 110, 113pp., 118, 121
Tokamahamon 105p., 108, 113, 115p.
Truro, Massachusetts. 40, 44, 49, 103
United States of America...........5, 15
Wampanoag................86, 96, 98, 107
Warren, Rhode Island............98, 102
Warren, Richard..........................52
Wellfleet, Massachusetts.................54
Wellfleet Bay & Harbor..............54p.
Whales......................28, 49, 54p.
White, Susanna..............................51
White, William.............................82
Winslow, Edward: biography, 5; 14, 17, 49, 52, 83, 90, 93, 96, 122, 128
Winslow, Elizabeth..................19, 83
Winthrop, John............................15
Wolves.................................56, 79

Sources

The Text —
The *Mayflower Report, 1622* is based on the popularly titled *Mourt's Relation*, a travelogue written by the Mayflower Pilgrims William Bradford and Edward Winslow, *et al.* The book's formal title is *A Relation or Journall* [sic] *of the beginning and proceedings of the English Plantation setled* [sic] *at Plimoth in New England* (London: John Bellamie, 1622).

However, the precise itinerary of the Pilgrims is often difficult to confirm because most places in America then had no English names. Nevertheless, a reasonable conjecture of places visited by the Pilgrims is in *Mourt's Relation or Journal of the Plantation at Plymouth, with an Introduction and Notes,* edited by Henry Martyn Dexter (Boston: John Kimball Wiggin, 1865); Dr. Dexter convincingly matches Pilgrim descriptions of landmarks with modern features. His map of Pilgrim travels on Cape Cod is reprinted in Volume III of *Narrative and Critical History of America,* edited by Justin Winsor (Boston: Houghton Mifflin, 1884), page 270. *The History of Plymouth Plantation, 1620-1647* also provides good background, being a richly annotated memoir by William Bradford, as edited by Worthington Chauncey Ford (Boston: Massachusetts Historical Society, 1912). Two other versions of Mr. Bradford's memoir, *Of Plymouth Plantation* edited by Samuel Eliot Morison (New York: Knopf, 1989) and *Bradford's History of Plymouth Plantation* edited by William T. Davis (New York: Charles Scribner's Sons, 1908), also contain useful annotation.

Illustrations —
Engravings, prints, and maps are based on nineteenth and early twentieth-century interpretations, including detailed land surveys by the U.S. government. Many were digitally restored and/or modified for this edition. Images include rare prints from the Library of Congress and engravings of wildlife from the Dover Pictorial Archive, a series of design books by Dover Publishing of Mineola, New York.

The map of Southern New England in 1634 is from *The History of North America, Volume V, The Colonization of New England* by James Bartlett Burleigh (Philadelphia: G. Barrie, 1904); John Goodwin's street map of Plymouth Colony is from his book, *The Pilgrim Republic* (Boston: Houghton Mifflin, 1920); and the facsimile of the original title page of *Mourt's Relation* is from *Bradford's History of Plymouth Plantation* edited by William T. Davis (see above).

www.ingramcontent.com/pod-product-compliance
Lightning Source LLC
Chambersburg PA
CBHW051803040426
42446CB00007B/501